THE FATHER LOVES YOU

Ed Piorek

VINEYARD INTERNATIONAL PUBLISHING

In loving memory of
John Wimber
– the man who led me to the Father.

VINEYARD INTERNATIONAL PUBLISHING
PO Box 53286
Kenilworth, 7745
Cape Town, South Africa
Email: vip@vineyardbi.org

First published 1999, Vineyard International Publishing
Re-published 2003, Vineyard International Publishing
Third publication 2005, Vineyard International Publishing

Cover by Mercy Arts Studio, USA
Printed and bound by ABC Press, Cape Town.

ISBN 0-620-24261-2

CONTENTS

Contents

ACKNOWLEDGMENTS

Fifteen years ago the Lord put it upon my heart to write this book. I am grateful to all who have helped bring this desire to fruition.

I would like to thank Ken Blue for encouraging me to begin this undertaking, and Derek Morphew for cheering me on to finish it.

I am deeply grateful to my secretary, Genesis Hansen, who contributed to this book through her research, supplemental writing, editing, and most of all her heartfelt devotion to the message of the Father's love.

I thank my wife, Janet, for always being there to support me in the sometimes challenging process of discovering the Father's love in my life and sharing this message through our conference ministry.

To my three sons, Brandon, Nathan, and David, thanks for being "arrows of the Father's love" that so faithfully find their mark in my heart.

Special thanks to the Vineyard Christian Fellowship of Mission Viejo for allowing me the time to work on this project and to all who have so generously supported this effort with their financial gifts.

I

THE SEARCH

*"The deepest search in life, it seemed to me, the thing
that in one way or another was central to all living was
man's search to find a father, not merely the father of
his flesh, not merely the lost father of his youth, but the
image of a strength and wisdom external to his need
and superior to his hunger, to which the belief and
power of his own life could be united." – Thomas Wolfe*

"Hit the glove!" I still remember the words my dad yelled
to me from behind the home plate of our practice baseball field in the empty lot beside my childhood home.
"Come on, son, throw a strike!" he called out as he centered the big catcher's mitt over the exact center of the
plate. I wound up and fired a pitch at the target. It was
very important to hit the glove, especially on that particular day. We had just returned from a Little League baseball game and things had not gone well.

I pitched the game and we lost. My father was the coach of the team and he was not too pleased with my performance. As we fell behind in the early innings I watched my dad's frown deepen. By the end of the game we were losing badly, and he began to verbalize his displeasure towards my performance, shouting instructions at me from the dugout. I was failing to "hit the glove." As I stood all alone out on the pitchers mound, my eyes filled with tears.

After the game we drove silently home. Upon arrival my dad got his catcher's mitt out of the trunk of the car, tossed me a baseball, and led me out to practice. In time I started finding the strike zone. "That's it, son!" responded my dad. "You have to throw strikes if you want to win!" And I wanted to win, especially in my father's eyes.

Winning was very important to my father. In the game of life he achieved considerable success at a relatively young age. He endured harsh Canadian winters supervising a rough bunch of bridge-building steelworkers and then parlayed his sizeable earnings into a successful real estate business in Southern California. I was his son and he genuinely wanted me to be successful also. He was generous with material "necessities" like new bicycles and baseball gloves, encouraging my extra-curricular activities. Whenever I needed help with my algebra or finding the right grip for a curveball, he was there. He imparted to me the vision that if a Piorek tried hard enough he could do anything. I loved my dad; he was a winner. Boy, did I want to be a winner like him. A son he could be proud of. A son that he could love.

My father's love was what I was looking for. Like all children, I loved my dad and opened up my heart to receive his love in return. However, the demonstration of affection I desired never came. Like most men of his generation, my father never learned how to be affectionate. He and his contemporaries were taught that men didn't display their emotions; men were supposed to demonstrate their feelings for their family by taking good care of them, providing for them. Michael Murphy, author of *Popsicle Fish,* a book of essays on fathering, remembers that his dad was "primarily focused on issues of survival and support ... he didn't spend much time with us, he wasn't affectionate, and I was afraid of him. Fathers in that day and age tended to be distant and weren't trained to be affectionate."[1] I can't remember my father ever saying "I love you" to me, or hugging me affectionately. I felt rejected and alone, with an emotional void that only deepened over the years.

From an early age I attempted to do whatever was necessary to get my father to express his love for me. By the time I was ten years old I was trying to throw strikes and hit the glove to earn his approval. Unfortunately, on more than one important occasion I missed, and instead of commendation received a firm corrective word that increased my sense of rejection. As the years passed, each experience of falling short was another brick in a wall of pain that separated me from others, and my loneliness grew. I was terrified of failure. When it came time for me to leave home, I took my fear and emptiness and my longing for a father's love, and tried to fill the void with what the big world out there had to offer.

The Search of a Fatherless Generation

I remember many a warm, California summer night in the 1960's, hanging out with the surfers and surfer girls, beer flowing, the party in full swing. It seemed to be the perfect setting for a young man trying to soothe his aching loneliness. I thought I could fill the void in my life with the camaraderie of the gang, the warm touch of a tanned California girl, the elevated sense of well-being brought on by a cool beer. On my own for the first time in my life, this was the lifestyle I chose. The little boy in me cried out for love, but I didn't know where to find it. Like the prodigal son of biblical fame, I tried to ease the pain in my heart with the shallow, sensual pleasures of the world around me. And, like him, I found that the sensual lifestyle never satisfied my need for the love of my father.

What it did was leave me empty, even more in touch with my deep need for love. As the prodigal son found himself on the road back to his father's home, I found myself on the sovereign road to finding the love of a greater Father – the Father whose love answered the plaintive cry of my heart.

We live in a society that is searching for the love of a father. The youth of today have been described as a "fatherless generation." It is a fitting term. David Blanken-horn, in his book *Fatherless America,* says:

> Tonight, about 40 percent of American children will go to sleep in homes in which their fathers do not live. Before they reach the age of eighteen, more than half of our nation's children are likely to spend at least a significant portion of their child-hoods living apart from their fathers.[2]

Many young people have poor relationships with their fathers. Some were abandoned physically or emotionally through a variety of circumstances: their parents divorced; their father's work schedule was too demanding and left him no time or energy for his family; their father was an alcoholic or a drug addict, completely absorbed in his own problems. They are searching to fill the emptiness created by the absence of a father's love. Others were rejected by their fathers. Perhaps they failed to live up to their father's standards of performance in school or sports; perhaps they were abused verbally, or even physically. These children cry out for the healing touch of a loving father to heal their wounds.

The father wounds which are acute in today's youth are also affecting many in our country's adult population. In a broad sense our entire society could be called "fatherless." As Blankenhorn says,

> … in addition to losing fathers, we are losing something larger: our idea of fatherhood. Unlike earlier periods of father absence in our history, we now face more than a physical loss affecting some homes. We face a cultural loss affecting every home.[3]

This cultural fatherlessness is evidenced by the prodigal lifestyles of many. Many choose to go to the party to find the love that is missing from their lives. Many try the "quick fixes" offered by alcohol, drugs, or immorality. But the need for a father's love is still there. The "sex, drugs and rock and roll" solution only leads to a discovery of emptiness and a reawakened desire to find father. The question then becomes: "How do we find him?"

"If you build it, he will come!" The words are a declaration of hope from the Kevin Costner hit movie *Field of Dreams.* They are the key to reconciliation with his dead father. Plowing under his cornfield to make a baseball diamond allows him a miraculous reunion with his father, a chance to express the words of love that eluded them in life. Tears rolled down my cheek as they played catch together, and I remembered my own dad playing catch with me. The movie was so powerful to me because it touched the nerve of my need to experience a father's love.

The heightened awareness of the need and desire to resolve the father issues of our lives is growing in our cultural expressions. Movies, pop music, novels, newspapers and magazines have all shown unprecedented interest in this subject, and often touch the same nerve of need for a father. In the Steven Spielberg movie *Hook,* Robin Williams plays Peter Pan as an adult. Not only an adult, but a man who has become so caught up in the concerns of his business and life that he has forgotten his magical childhood completely, and is completely out of touch with his own children. Their need for their father's love becomes a crucial issue in the movie.

Interestingly, when movies deal with father issues any healing touch of love that is offered is usually found in some sort of magical Hollywood encounter beyond the borders of real life. In *Hook,* Peter has to go back to Neverland and remember who he was before he can battle Captain Hook and get his children back. In the 1990 film version of *The Secret Garden,* the children build a bonfire and make up their own magical incantation to bring Colin's father back to him. Perhaps without really knowing it these movies are reflecting the search for a love that transcends this earthly existence, a love that comes from God. It is where my own search led.

A Searching Church

In the fall of 1967 I was called to the hospital where my mother was being treated for a serious form of cancer discovered only a few weeks earlier. When I reached her room I was stunned by the news that she had just passed away. For the next few days I was overpowered by the sense of loss. The little boy in me who already felt painfully distant from his dad suddenly realized that the one source of loving affection in his life was gone. I was frightened and alone. The night of my mother's burial, that fear rose up and surrounded me with its darkness. As I lay trembling in my bed, my thoughts turned to suicide.

Unknown to me, my wife sensed the ominous moment and prayed a simple prayer: "God, help us!" I will never forget the moment when I perceived a supernatural presence like a gentle wind enter the room. It touched me, alleviating my fear, and caused me miraculously to fall fast asleep. When I awoke the next morning I looked at my wife and said, "I met God last night!" She responded,

"So did I!" It happened to be Sunday morning so we decided to go to church. As we sang the first hymn I felt the presence again, and when I found myself singing about Jesus I realized it was him whom I had met in the night. I burst into tears as the Lord filled me with comfort over the loss of my mother. After a few weeks of attending church, my wife and I went to a Bible study where the concept of salvation was clarified for me and I formally gave my life to Jesus as Lord and Savior.

Several months after my conversion I was invited to teach a small Junior High Sunday School class. This was the beginning of years of zealous service for the Lord. My desire to serve was sincere, and my ministry was fruitful. However, my good intentions were tainted a little by a feeling of competitiveness. I was still insecure. Even though I had dramatically met Jesus, I knew little of the person and power of the Holy Spirit. I felt I had to rely on my own youthful energies to succeed in ministry. And when it came to knowing God the Father and his love, I was unable to get past the image of my dad, whose love seemed dependent on "hitting the glove." For the first fourteen years of my Christian life I tried to "hit the glove for God." I felt I had to study the Bible more diligently than others, pray more, witness more. My radical motto was "I would rather burn out than rust out." It wasn't long before my diligence and zeal propelled me ahead of others and into leadership, and soon enough I was standing behind the pulpit as pastor of my own church, wearing a three-piece suit and attempting to preach perfect three-point sermons.

Unfortunately, perfection is impossible to achieve, and the occasional criticism of well-meaning parishioners felt like arrows of rejection. All my experiences of letting my dad down left me with a deep-seated fear of failure, and those arrows of rejection always found their mark. When these emotions surfaced I harnessed them in a valiant attempt to do even better, but the increase of effort led to an early spiritual and emotional burnout. I needed more of God's enabling power in my life.

About this time, I went to a seminar on church growth where a leader in the field by the name of John Wimber was speaking. During his presentation he made an isolated comment that I found very interesting: "I have had the opportunity to lay hands on burned-out pastors and see them empowered by the Holy Spirit". Even though I came from a very conservative theological position concerning the ministry of the Holy Spirit in the church today, this statement went right to my heart and spoke to my need. Months later John did lay hands on me and my wife and we began a new season of ministry in the power of the Spirit. It was exciting to learn about the person of the Holy Spirit and use spiritual gifts. It was exciting to "do the stuff," a Wimber phrase for ministering like Jesus did: saving the lost, healing the sick and casting out demons. I did the stuff with the same zeal I used to preach my sermons in the preceding years. Although I experienced great success in my re-energized ministry, the nagging fear of failure was still there. I still had not come to know my loving Father in heaven. I was still trying to hit the glove. I was still searching for a father's love.

In his book called *The Forgotten Father*, Anglican theologian Thomas Smail writes:

> when one widens the scope and looks at vital modern Christian movements of any kind, one has to admit that emphasis upon and devotion to the Father has not been a main characteristic of many of them. Evangelicals have been concerned chiefly with Christ the Son, his divine person, his adequate atonement, his real resurrection and have of course not denied, but not made much of the fact that the Son is only the Son because he comes from the Father.
>
> Charismatics on the other hand have often switched the emphasis from the Son to the Spirit as the sovereign source of renewal, power and spiritual gifts and fruit. … It is now perhaps a little more clear in what sense I can justify my title and say that the Father has been "forgotten" – not of course in the sense that he has been doctrinally denied. He has

been regularly and ritually confessed, but his being and work as Father has been out of the centre of concern.[4]

"Forgotten," "out of the centre of concern" – these are phrases that certainly describe my relationship to God as Father in the first eighteen years of my Christian life, phrases that would fit the experience of many in the church today. Why is this so? Probably due to a simple lack of information. Teaching about the Fatherhood of God and particularly about the experience of his love is strangely absent from the church. Using the word adoption for the experience of God's love, J. I. Packer writes:

> It is a strange fact that the truth of adoption has been little regarded in Christian history. Apart from two last-century books, now scarcely known … there is no evangelical writing on it, nor has there been at any time since the Reformation, any more than there was before.[5]

I discovered during my years in conservative evangelical churches that there is an abundance of rich teaching, but when God as Father is discussed the language usually drifts toward the theological and away from the personal. For years the thought of the Father quickly brought to mind terms like sovereign, holy, omnipotent, eternal – terms that were true, but seemed to crowd out any real awareness of his tender, compassionate nature. The concept of God as Father got lost amidst the theological language. It is a serious loss. As Packer says:

> You sum up the whole of New Testament religion if you describe it as the knowledge of God as one's holy Father. If you want to judge how well a person understands Christianity, find out how much he makes of the thought of being God's child, and having God as his Father. If this is not the thought that prompts and controls his worship and prayers and his whole outlook on life, it means that he does not understand Christianity very well at all. For everything that Christ taught, everything that makes the New Testament new, and better than the Old, everything that is distinctively Christian as opposed to merely Jewish, is summed up in the knowledge of the Fatherhood of God. "Father" is the Christian name for God.[6]

Charles Stanley, pastor of First Baptist Church in Atlanta, Georgia, came to realize this theological blind spot when he finally was awakened to the Father's love. At one point in his life he became desperate to be free from deep feelings of rejection that seemed to be rooted in the loss of his father when he was seven months old. Several friends ministered to him, and he describes what happened:

One of these fellows said, "Charles, put your head on the table and close your eyes." So I did. Then he said to me very kindly, "Charles, your father just picked you up in his arms and held you. What do you feel?" I burst out crying. And I cried and I cried, and I could not stop crying. Finally, when I stopped, he asked me again, and I said that I felt warm and loved and secure and good, and I started weeping again. For the first time in my life I felt God emotionally loving me. All these years I had preached about trusting God and believing him and obeying him. And I had. But I came back and I looked through my sermon file, and in all of those years I had only preached one sermon on the love of God and it was not worth listening to. The reason was because I didn't know what it meant to feel the love of God because my daddy had walked out on me in death at seven months of age.[7]

Even when I became involved with the more charismatic segments of the church I did not easily discover the Father and his love. When I experienced the powerful presence of the Holy Spirit, my emotions were moved and my tears flowed. People prayerfully affirmed that the Spirit was resting on me, but no one pointed out that the Father was there at that very moment touching me with his love. It seems that many charismatic Christians forget to look for the face of the Father in their spiritual experiences. When we fail to perceive the Father in the midst of our Christian experience we then fail to appropriate the touch of his love we are desperately searching for. The result is that, although we may know God has touched us, our souls remain insecure and our deep inner search continues.

Several years ago, a very distraught young man came to me for some counsel and prayer. He was a martial arts instructor in the process of opening his own studio and was extremely anxious over this new endeavor. I found it strange that this muscular powerhouse of a man would be so fearful. He explained that he grew up as the son of a Pentecostal minister, in a church that often prophesied that he would fill his father's shoes. Growing up and becoming the owner of a martial arts studio filled him with the fear of disappointing the hopes of his father and the church. He was desperate to experience the love and acceptance of his Father in heaven in order to move ahead in his own life. As I prayed for him to receive the Father's love, the Holy Spirit touched him powerfully and he burst into tears. After several minutes he looked up at me and queried "When will I ever experience the Father's love?" I asked him what he thought he was experiencing right then as he was weeping. He said he was experiencing the power of the Holy Spirit just as he had so many times before in Pentecostal church meetings. As he spoke I realized that he had never perceived the involvement of his heavenly Father in his many infillings of the Holy Spirit and as a result he failed to appropriate the love that could alleviate his insecurity. When I simply informed him that the Father was there and touching him, he burst into tears again, this time reaching out and calling, "Father! Oh, thank you, Father". This time the flow of the Spirit was received as the warm embrace of a loving father and he was secured and set free to embark on the adventure of his life.

As Thomas Wolfe states, the search to find a father is "the deepest search in life". We begin early in our childhood seeking to connect with our fathers and be loved by them. When this doesn't happen we begin to search the offerings of the world around us to fill the void. Ultimately, however, there is nothing in the world that can take the place of a father's love. Our pursuit will leave us emptier than when we started. Even if our childhood experience of father was relatively good, something from eternity beckons us to come and receive a love far more fulfilling.

We find this love through Jesus, the man who made the incredible statement, "I am the way, the truth, and the life. No man comes to the Father but by me." When we come to accept Jesus as our Savior we need to remind ourselves that Jesus wants to introduce us to his Father so that we can find the love we are looking for. Jesus helps us to include a loving Father in our theological perception of God and see the face of the Father in our experiences in the Holy Spirit. Our first encounter with his love invites us to fully come to know him as Abba Father and experience his affectionate love to the core of our being.

2

HEAT-SEEKING MISSILES

"Jesus is the Blessed One. When Jesus was baptized in the Jordan River a voice came from heaven saying, 'You are my Son, the Beloved; my favor rests on you' (Mark 1:11). This was the blessing that sustained Jesus during his life. ... Jesus came into the world to share that blessing with us." – Henri Nouwen

When our son David was about six or seven years old we referred to him as our "heat-seeking missile." A heat-seeking missile is an armed projectile that zeroes in on its target by sensing the heat that is emitted from its engines. David came into this nickname as a result of behavior we observed around the house. Playing by himself while Janet and I were busy elsewhere in the house, he occasionally became alarmed, aware of being alone. Whenever this happened he left his play and came in search of us. On more than one occasion his quest coincided with a moment when Janet and I were sharing a spontaneous kiss. In the midst of our embrace we heard the sound of little feet coming down the hallway and then the door burst open as David rushed in. He wedged his body between us and looked up.

When I saw that little cherub face I realized what he was looking for. He had become frightened and was looking for the assurance of being safe in our loving presence. Now David knew in his head that we loved him, for we often told him. But at this moment in his young life he needed to experience it in his anxious heart. He was like a heat-seeking missile in search of the warmth of love. So I took his upturned head in my hands and said, "David, we love you." Then I hugged him and held him closely for a while. You could almost hear the meter running as his tank was filled with love. Then, just as suddenly as he came, he broke loose and ran back to his play. The missile had found its mark.

Heat-seeking missiles! It's a term that could describe all of us. We grow up seeking the heat of affectionate love. We look first to our parents, especially our fathers. If we get the love we are looking for from our fathers our tanks are filled with the warm liquid of love and our heart is secured. If we cannot connect with the targeted love we go through life trying to find it in other relationships.

However, the original father emptiness remains and even the best relationships cannot fill the tank. Many of us eventually come to the realization that the sought-after embrace still eludes us. Often we begin to search for this love beyond our natural sphere. We head down the hall-way of life and begin looking for God the Father.

This is the way God has built us. We were created by our Father in heaven with a need to know his love. We will never be really secure in this life until we bury our-selves in the warm embrace of his loving arms. Even as Christians we can find that this experience is missing from our lives. We may know intellectually that the Father loves us but our deep insecurities tell us that we must have more. After years of being a Christian I found myself looking for the room where I could open the door and run into my Father's waiting presence.

In His Steps

In the early eighties, I was assisting John Wimber in his seminars by teaching on the healing ministry of Jesus. The material I used was developed by John, and brought out the importance of the relationship Jesus had with his Father. In his life and ministry Jesus revealed a radically new understanding of God as Father. He startled the prevalent Jewish mindset by addressing God as "Abba", an intimate term of endearment used by children with their fathers.[1] In doing so, he not only showed us the nature of his relationship with the Father but the potential for us with the Father if we follow in the footsteps of Jesus the Son.

When questioned by the Jews in John chapter 5 as to why he healed the invalid on the Sabbath, Jesus told them he was working on the Sabbath because his Father was working on the Sabbath. He went on to say something that I found both informative and challenging: "I tell you the truth, the Son can do nothing by himself; he can do only what he sees his Father doing, because whatever the Father does the Son also does" (John 5:19).

This statement reveals the dependence Jesus had on an intimate relationship with his Father. An obedient Son who wanted to do the Father's will, he needed to stay close to his Father and hear his voice of direction. What a challenge to us as modern Christians! If we want to achieve anything of value in his kingdom, we must know the Father. If Jesus the Divine Son could do nothing apart from relationship with the Father, how much less will we do without him? That thought caused me some anxiety, because I never felt entirely sure that the Father would show me what he was doing. But then I had another thought: perhaps in his humanity Jesus, who showed the full range of emotions during his time on earth, also felt some anxiety during challenging times of ministry. What would calm his heart and keep him quietly secured so that he could wait to hear from his Father? The Bible tells us that it was the knowledge of his Father's love. In John 5:20 it says, "For the Father loves the Son and shows him all he does." These words sank deeply into my searching heart.

We are looking for a love that touches our hearts; a demonstrated, natural affection. First we look to our natural fathers and then to our Father in heaven. Examining the specific language of the Bible provides further insight into this affectionate love, for when we read that "the Father loves the Son," the Greek word used for love is *phileo.* This is the root word that appears in the name of the city of Philadelphia, the city of brotherly love, and it is meant to convey the affection demonstrated between friends and family members. It is a word to describe the *experience* of love.

Most Christians are familiar with another well-known Greek word for love, *agape,* used in the Bible to convey God's unconditional love for us. It is used in verses like Romans 5:8 where we are told that "God demonstrated his love [*agape*] for us in that while we were still sinners Christ died for us." In texts like this we see a loving Father-God in heaven making a sovereign decision to send his Son down to earth to be with us and die for us so that we might be saved and join them one day in heaven.

31

Often *agape* describes loving transactions made by our Father at some distance. But when the Bible describes God's love coming close to us and actually touching our hearts, *phileo* is the word that is used. *In Vine's Expository Dictionary of New Testament Words* the author comments: "*PHILEO* is to be distinguished from *agape* in this, that *phileo* more nearly represents tender affection."[2] Thus we see that Jesus had a relationship with his Father in heaven where he experienced his demonstrated, natural affection. If we take a closer look at some of the memorable events in the life of Jesus, I believe we can see this affectionate love in them, and his experience of love can become ours.

The baptism of Jesus is one of those events that the gospel writers thought so significant that all four record it. If we look at it with eyes to see the Father's love in it, it becomes a dramatic illustration of what that love was like in the life experience of Jesus. Let's look at the account of Mark:

> At that time Jesus came from Nazareth in Galilee and was baptized by John in the Jordan. As Jesus was coming up out of the water, he saw heaven being torn open and the Spirit descending on him like a dove. And a voice came from heaven: "You are my Son, whom I love; with you I am well pleased" (Mark 1:9–11).

The baptism of Jesus marks his public acceptance of the work of redeeming mankind by identifying with their sin and committing himself to sacrifice his life for them on the cross. When I think about Jesus as a man with emotions like ours, contemplating this challenging future, I can see why, as the gospel of Luke tells us, he prays to his Father upon emerging from the Jordan. And immediately heaven is torn open as if by unseen hands, the Spirit descends upon him and the Father speaks into his ears words of assurance. Bible commentator Norval Geldenhuys elaborates:

> after Jesus had now offered Himself so completely and voluntarily as the Substitute and Redeemer, God gave to His human consciousness a perfect revelation of the majesty and glory of the Father, and of the fact that He was the Son of God in an absolute sense. ... This opening of the heaven, the descent of the Holy Ghost in a visible shape, and the voice from heaven, were to Jesus the final assurance from God that He was indeed His Son and the anointed Messiah.[3]

The Father's voice not only confirms Jesus as his Son and chosen Servant, but goes beyond these Messianic titles (found in Psalm 2:7 and Isaiah 42:1, respectively) by calling him "the Beloved."[4] In using this special term of endearment, which happens to be *agapetos* in the original Greek, the Father reminds the Son of his love for him and reveals to the watching world a new and tender dimension of that love.

The Father gave Jesus the reassurance that his human heart required. It came through the touch of the Father's manifest presence and loving words. In this instance we can see the *philia* love of the Father; his demonstrated, natural affection for his Son. The three most powerful words in the English language are "I love you." If we hear them from our fathers when we are young they have a powerful effect for good. If we don't, the insecurities that result can severely undermine our success in life. Jesus heard those powerful words of love and his heart was secured. He could say absolutely: "Yes, I am my Father's Son! Yes, he loves me!"

This experience of the Father's love proved to be of critical importance in the life of Jesus. When Satan attempted to detour Jesus from his mission he did so by tempting him to prove his Sonship. But Jesus didn't need to prove himself by turning stones into bread; he relied on every word that his Father spoke, and his Father had made it clear that Jesus was his son and that he loved him. As Henri Nouwen points out, "Jesus, however, is very clear in his response: 'I don't have to prove that I am worthy of love. I am the Beloved of God, the One on whom God's favor rests.'"⁵ How often the enemy tempts us to do things to prove our self-worth. To avoid temptation in those moments we need the same experience that Jesus had; an experience of demonstrated love that secures our hearts.

From his baptism on, Jesus was never even an arm's length away from his Father who loved him. The ears that heard the words "I love you" were attentive to every direction for every challenging situation. As we face the challenges of life we also need to have a sensitivity to the voice of our Father. Listening to the Father requires a heart secured by the same words that Jesus heard: "I love you!"

We get glimpses of this ongoing love relationship between the Father and the Son throughout the gospels. On the Mount of Transfiguration the cloud of the Father's presence surrounded Jesus and again the Father spoke of his love for his Son. Later, in the Garden of Gethsemane, Jesus voiced his response to his Father's loving presence in his "Abba, Father" cry. As we look into the life of Jesus and see how his relationship with his Father helped him to fulfill his purpose, we are challenged to examine our own experiences with the Father. When I examined my life, I realized that I needed to go back to the beginning – back to standing alongside Jesus on the banks of the Jordan and praying to the Father, "Father, reassure me of your love for me!" Like my son David, I was a heat-seeking missile looking for the warm affection of my Father's touch. At some point in our lives I believe most of us come to that same realization.

The Touch of Love

During the last evening the disciples spent with the Lord Jesus before his crucifixion I believe that they, too, became heat-seeking missiles. In the upper room Jesus broke the news to them that he would soon be leaving. As if that was not enough to make them feel insecure, he also told them that when he left they would go on to do even greater works then he. I can imagine the panic and anxiety the disciples must have felt. It must have been very difficult for them to believe that they would do greater works than Jesus! I picture them forming a "holy huddle" of sorts, and asking each other "What in the world are we going to do?" Perhaps they looked back over the time they spent with Jesus, looking for his secrets of successful ministry. One of them probably realized that Jesus was constantly in communication with his Father, and his Father would direct him toward the things he wanted done. With this in mind, they might have asked him, "How do we know that your Father will answer us after you're gone and we ask him to show us what he wants us to do and how to do it?" John records a perfect answer to such a question: "In that day you will ask in my name. I am not saying that I will ask the Father on your behalf. No, the Father himself loves you because you have loved me and have believed that I came from God" (John 16: 26–27).

Jesus promised direct access to the Father when we come in his name. Even more amazing is the revelation that when we love Jesus we can receive the love of his Father. The Greek word used here for love is the same one we saw earlier in John 5:20 – *phileo*. Jesus promised that the same demonstrated, natural affection that he experienced from his Father was available to everyone who placed their faith in him. This promise was very meaningful to the fearful disciples for they were well aware of the nature of the love between Jesus and his Father. Jesus gave them the hope that the Father would pour the same securing love into their hearts that he had received at his baptism. They had hope that the Father would show them how to successfully carry on the work of his Son. And as with all of the promises spoken by Jesus, this also applies to those of us today who have come to know and love him.

Jesus' desire that each person who comes to love him will experience the wonderful love of his Father is evident in his prayer in John 17:

> "Righteous Father, though the world does not know
> you, I know you, and they know that you have sent

> me. I have made you known to them, and will con-
> tinue to make you known in order that the love you
> have for me may be in them and that I myself may
> be in them" (John 17:25–26).

This passage refers to those who have come to realize that
Jesus is the Christ, the Son of the living God, and it refers
specifically to the original disciples. However, this por-
tion of the prayer includes all believers, extending to us
today. Jesus said that he made the Father known to these
original followers through his incarnate life and ministry.
Earlier that evening he told the disciples that if they had
seen him they had seen the Father. In this passage he
states that he will continue to make the Father known to
them until they come to experience fully the same love
that he himself experienced from his Father. On this
ongoing revelation of the Father's love B. F. Westcott
comments:

> This revelation, complete in one sense *(I made
> known),* is none the less continuous *(I will make
> known).* It cannot be finished while the world lasts.
> The end of it is that the Father may regard the dis-
> ciples in response to their growing faith even as He
> regarded the Son, and that they may feel His love.[6]

If there is one prayer that I believe the Father will defi-
nitely answer it is the prayer of his Son. He prayed that

the men in the upper room would come to experience the love of their heavenly Father, and this prayer was dramatically answered on the day of Pentecost when the Spirit brought the fulfillment of the Father's promises. The first installment of this promised love also became mine as I put my faith in these newly discovered truths in the Word of God.

In 1985 my travels with John Wimber led me to Oklahoma City where nearly 1500 people were gathered for a conference on the subject of healing. This was not my first healing conference with John. I often assisted him in his seminars while he discipled me in doing the works of Jesus. He had a unique model for training. While he gave an inspiring message about Jesus' passion to heal the sick, I'd sit in the audience cheering him on. Then he would invite someone forward who needed to receive prayer for healing. Sometimes the conditions were very serious like blindness or an obvious physical deformity. I admired his courage to pray for healing in front of so many people. Just about the time I sat up in my seat, not wanting to miss the action, John would make this very disturbing statement: "In order to show you that Jesus can use any of us to accomplish his healing works, I would like Eddie to come up and pray for this person." Instantly my heart was overwhelmed with the fear of failing in front of everyone. Would I be able to "hit the glove"? I'd wipe away the revealing beads of sweat and attempt to keep my composure as I stepped up to the stage. Mean-while, my heart would cry out my best "Lord help me!" prayer. To my amazement he often healed the needy person, but the anxiety of these moments took its toll on me and I soon realized that I had to find a better way to deal with my terrible fears.

When I discovered the promise that the Father loves me with the same *philia* love as his son Jesus, I wanted to appropriate that love in my life. I began to use self-talk. On the way up to the stage to pray for people I would tell myself, "The Father loves me. He will show me what he is doing." This helped me to suppress the rising fear long enough to get through the times of ministry, but I realized that a real experience of this love still eluded me.

In Oklahoma City the stage was set for a real breakthrough. On Friday night after the evening session John informed me that he had to head home early the next morning and that I would be on my own. At that moment I could really identify with the disciples on the night Jesus announced his imminent departure. After a fitful night's sleep I went out jogging to run off my mounting anxiety. When I returned I slipped into the relaxing waters of a steaming outdoor Jacuzzi. As soon as I leaned back and gazed up into the blue morning sky I saw a large jet aeroplane flying overhead. Checking my watch I realized that John Wimber was on that plane returning home. The knot in my stomach was instantaneous as I was gripped by the fearful vision of having to take John's place in front of that large crowd.

I lifted my hands up to heaven and began the self-talk. "Father, your word says that you love me and will show me what to do. Father, I need your love right now!" Suddenly I felt a warm presence flood my body, seemingly targeted at the anxious knot. When it found its mark I felt immediate relief and began to cry. My first thought was to ask, "What was that?" and the answer which was impressed on my mind was, "This is the Father's love for you." When I finished crying I was filled with a sense of peace, and went on to a wonderful time of ministry. As I look back on that moment in the Jacuzzi I realize that it marked my first identifiable experience of the Father's love. For the first time in my life I felt the warm embrace of a father's arms. As a heat-seeking missile I had finally hit my target.

In the years since then I have spoken to hundreds of people who like me had a very good theological understanding of the Father's love for them but had never experienced the touch of his love. While being able to expound on the great meaning of the word *agape*, many had missed the warmth of the Father's *philia* love in their life. After hearing the promise of this love to all who love

Jesus, many reached out to receive from the Father with a new expectancy. Many found the Father quick to draw near and touch them.

We are living in a time in history when the prayer of Jesus is being answered in a magnificent way. Jesus is revealing his loving Father to us so that we might know the same love he knows. After all, Jesus was not sent to save us so that we might be trophies of grace adorning some heavenly wall; he saved us to bring us back to our Father who has desired to hold us in his arms of love since before time began. Even today he is reaching out to heat-seeking missiles to say "I love you" and to secure you with his touch of love.

3

ABBA, FATHER

"If in my Father's love
I share a filial part,
Send down Thy Spirit like a dove
To rest upon my heart." – Charles Spurgeon

Whenever someone shares a testimony with me about experiencing the Father's love, I ask them to write it down. Periodically I go back to this file of testimonies – they are a source of great joy and encouragement to me. This testimony from a young California surfer by the name of Matt is one I've always treasured:

> After being saved for a few years, several friends and I went to one of their parents' property in the desert to goof around. ... The subject of baptism came up, and we realized to our surprise that three of the four in our group had never been baptized.

We decided to baptize each other. I never thought
of it as anything more than symbolic, so what happened next was the biggest surprise of my life. As I
came up out of the water, the presence of God fell
to earth around me. He became so real, and all at
once I was crying out to him, saying, "Daddy,
Daddy," instead of the formal "Father, Father." All
my life I have known of "Our Father who art in
heaven," but now he was my Daddy. I was melted
in his presence. All the while, my hands had what I
can only describe as 10,000 volts of electricity flowing out of them. It was as though I could weld steel
with a touch of my finger. Since that time, I have
never doubted that God is real, and that He loves
me.

Wow! 10,000 volts of electric love! While not everyone
will have an experience of this magnitude, Matt's experience does have all the component parts of the Father's
love we want to explore here. The Holy Spirit descends,
bringing a witness of the Father's love and evoking a deep
emotional response which causes us to address God intimately as Abba, Father. Our reception of the love the
Spirit brings is key to being embraced by the Father and
emotionally knowing and loving him.

The Spirit of Love

On the day of Pentecost the Holy Spirit descended on the apostles and disciples in the Upper Room. Most of us are aware that they received power to be witnesses for Christ (Acts 1:8). Charismatic Christians take special note of the fact that they received Spiritual gifts as evidenced by speaking in tongues (Acts 2:4). But hardly anyone takes note of the fact that the love of God the Father was also poured out on that special day. This is a serious oversight because the outpouring of the Spirit and the experience of the Father's love are vitally linked.

When the Apostle Paul first mentions the work of the Spirit in the book of Romans, he focuses on the experience of God's love: "And hope does not disappoint us, because God has poured out his love into our hearts by the Holy Spirit, whom he has given us" (Romans 5:5). James Dunn helps us to understand the significance of this verse when he says: "Paul uses vivid 'Pentecostal' language ('poured out in our hearts'), and obviously recalls his readers to deep emotional experiences which must have been common to many of those who became Christians at that time."[1]

Deep emotional experiences that were common to Christians in the early church? Evidently when the early Christians experienced the outpouring of the Spirit they had a paradigm that allowed them to see the Father's love in it. Sadly, I think that this paradigm has largely been lost in the church today, and must be regained if we are to experience the love of the Father in a real and tangible way.

This tangible experience of God's love is evident in many accounts of revivals in the history of the church. With the outpouring of the Spirit comes a new awareness of the experience of God's love. A classic example of this is found in the personal testimony of Charles Finney, the great evangelist in the Second Great Awakening. One evening in the Fall of 1821, Finney, a newly-converted lawyer, had this extraordinary experience:

> I returned to the front office, and found that the fire that I had made of large wood was nearly burned out. But as I turned and was about to take a seat by the fire, I received a mighty baptism of the Holy Ghost. Without any expectation if it, without ever having the thought in my mind that there was any such thing for me, without any recollection that I had ever heard the thing mentioned by any person in the world, the Holy Ghost descended on me in a manner that seemed to go through me, body and soul. I could feel the impression, like a wave of electricity, going through and through me. Indeed it seemed to come in waves and waves of liquid love; for I could not express it in any other

way. It seemed like the very breath of God. I can recollect distinctly that it seemed to fan me, like immense wings.

No words can express the wonderful love that was shed abroad in my heart. I wept aloud with joy and love; and I do not know but I should say, I literally bellowed out the unutterable gushings of my heart. The waves came over me, and over me, one after the other, until I recollect I cried out, "I shall die if these waves continue to pass over me." I said, "Lord, I cannot bear any more;" yet I had no fear of death.[2]

Finney's statement, "No words can express the wonderful love that was shed abroad in my heart" is apparently a spontaneous quote of our Romans verse. How similar his experience is to our young California surfer's! This should not surprise us because the Spirit who touched these men with the Father's love is the same Spirit that descended on the church at Pentecost to empower them and fill them with the Father's love. And through this outpouring of the Spirit individual believers come to experience what Jesus experienced at his baptism. Clark Pinnock, in his book *Flame of Love,* describes the progression nicely:

In baptism [Jesus] experienced God as his Father and was conscious of his own sonship. ... The Pentecost event parallels the baptism of Jesus – the disciples were baptized and empowered for mission, as Jesus had been in the Jordan. … Christ took the representative journey on behalf of all human beings, and now the Spirit is drawing people into it, making the mission of the representative existentially effective by pouring the love of God into our hearts. … We have been adopted into a filial relationship with the Father, as Jesus was in the Jordan.[3]

We who have become his disciples have the hope of receiving this outpouring of love when we reach out for the promise of Pentecost to be fulfilled in our lives today. A woman named Lynn nearly lost her hope after years of persevering against a debilitating bone disease. She has had numerous broken bones, been in eleven body casts, and for the past seventeen years has been in a wheelchair. When Lynn experienced a time of severe difficulty and rejection at work, she said:

Somehow the pain of being disabled seemed to surface as well. I felt rejected by God because I had been born with this condition and he had not healed me.

I was so angry and bitter that it scared me. I wasn't sure if my faith would survive the intensity of the pain I felt. Then one night, as some friends prayed for me, I saw myself in a valley of bitterness. There were skeletons lying in the dirt around me and I realized many people had become stuck in this bitter place and died. I was afraid I would die there, too. I cried out to the Father to rescue me because I didn't know the way out. I felt trapped in bitterness.

Suddenly the Father came and I felt the warmth of his love going through my body. There was a physical sensation much like electricity, but it was very sweet. I lost track of time. I forgot where I was and who was praying for me. I was in the presence of the Lord and the Father was holding me in his arms. My head was nestled against his chest and I wept and cried there as I poured out my disappointment.

Then, as another wave of love went through my body, I began to laugh with great joy. Nothing funny was said, I hadn't thought about laughing, but when his touch went through me again I started to laugh heartily. The Lord said to me, "A joyful heart is strength to the bones," and his joy was filling me.

The Father took the pain of rejection and secured me in his love again. He gave me the power to face the difficult circumstances in my work and in being in my wheelchair. Most of all, I received the precious gift of the Father's love. Through such times, I realize he is what I want and what I really need, anyway.

In Lynn's testimony we hear the echo of the words of Charles Finney. God's love moved through them like electricity as they poured out their hearts in his presence. It is this experience of love that we all deeply desire. It is this experience of love that Paul speaks of when he discusses adoption.

Evidence of Adoption

It has been said that the Apostle Paul's loftiest theological work is contained in the book of Romans. If that is true, then the highest peak of the mountains of truth is Chapter 8, with the snow-capped summit these verses:

> because those who are led by the Spirit of God are sons of God. For you did not receive a spirit that makes you a slave again to fear, but you received the Spirit of sonship. And by him we cry, "Abba, Father." The Spirit himself testifies with our spirit that we are God's children. Now if we are children, then we are heirs – heirs of God and co-heirs with Christ, if indeed we share in his sufferings in order that we may also share in his glory (Romans 8: 14–17).

In Romans 5:5 we were told that the Spirit pours out the love of God in our hearts. In Romans 8 Paul gives us an even clearer picture of the work the Spirit does in our hearts to convince us that we are the children of a loving heavenly Father.

Paul seeks in the book of Romans to give a theological explanation of the gospel of God in which we are saved through faith and not works. His primary point is that sinful mankind can be saved through faith in Jesus. But Paul emphasizes that the full benefit of the gospel is that saved men and women are sons and daughters of their heavenly Father, having been adopted in Christ. Our salvation has an important relational aspect. We have been saved by a Father who wants us to come into intimate relationship with him, even as his Son Jesus knew. The Spirit works in our lives to make this coming into the embrace of God a relational reality. Pinnock states:

> When we look at salvation from the standpoint of the Spirit, we view it in relational, affective terms. … Spirit is leading us to union – to transforming, personal, intimate relationship with the triune God. … Salvation is directed toward the loving embrace of God. … Spirit is bringing us into intimacy with the Father through the Son. … Believers, in Christ by the Spirit, are beginning to participate in God and experience the love pouring from the Father to the Son.[4]

The goal of the Spirit is to make our adoption a reality in

our lives, a reality that is anchored in a vital experience of the Father's love.

Paul begins with the statement that his Christian readers have received the Spirit of adoption. James Dunn interprets this as "the spirit which effects adoption or the spirit which expresses adoption."[5] In other words, the Spirit makes our adoption real. The Greek word for adoption is *huio-thesia,* which literally means "the placing as a son" and was a legal term used in the Greco-Roman culture at the time of Paul. H. A. Ironside describes the cultural event of adoption:

> When a Roman father publicly acknowledged his child as his son and heir, legally in the forum, this ceremony was called "the adoption!" All born in his family were children. Only those adopted were recognized as sons.[6]

The language used here describes what the Spirit effects: bringing us into the presence of our heavenly Father to be given tangible evidence that we are his own. That this evidence is of an experiential nature can be inferred from the very strong language describing the response of the one adopted. Paul states that we cry out "Abba, Father" as a result. This cry is one of intimacy and intensity. Henri Nouwen focuses on its intimacy in his devotional book *Bread for the Journey:*

The Spirit reveals to us not only that God is "Abba, Father" but also that we belong to God as beloved children. The Spirit thus restores in us the relationship from which all other relationships derive their meaning.

Abba is a very intimate word. The best translation for it is "Daddy." The word Abba expresses trust, safety, confidence, belonging, and most of all, intimacy. It does not have the connotation of authority, power, and control that the word Father often evokes. On the contrary, Abba implies an embracing and nurturing love. This love includes and infinitely transcends all the love that comes to us from our fathers, mothers, brothers, sisters, spouses, friends, and lovers. It is the gift of the Spirit.[7]

Dunn elaborates on the intensity of the experience:

What Paul has in mind cannot, however, be reduced to a merely inner sense, a quiet conviction of sonship. The verb used ("cry out") implies an intensity of feeling or fervor of expression. And its inclusion in the established formula (Gal 4:6) implies that such intensity was a regular feature of the uttered phrase.[8]

In his epic work on Romans, Martin Lloyd-Jones further amplifies the meaning of "crying out":

These are the very words used by our Lord at the time of His great agony. He used them when He was sweating great drops of blood. This is the cry He uttered, 'Abba, Father.' And that is the very cry, the Apostle tells us, that comes out of the heart of the one who realizes that he has been adopted as a child of God.[9]

What does the Spirit do to invoke such a deep emotional response? The answer lies in verse 16. Here is the verse again with comments on the intensity of this witness from James Dunn:

"The Spirit itself bears witness with our spirit that we are children of God." It is presumable this same intense consciousness of sonship expressed in the cry "Abba, Father" which Paul still has in mind – a sense that it is not just himself praying but his inner being enabled to pray by the enabling of God.[10]

The Holy Spirit touches us in such a way that we have an "intense consciousness of sonship." Martin Lloyd-Jones elaborates further on the witness of the Spirit and gives us a hint of the essential nature of this experience:

This is something subjective, something which essentially belongs to the realm of feeling and sub-jectivity, and the emotions. ... Paul is really telling

us that we are to feel – and I am emphasizing feeling – in this sense, what our Lord Himself felt.[11]

When he says we are to feel what our Lord himself felt,
he is referring to Jesus' experience when he received the
evidence of his Father's love at his baptism. Dunn agrees:

> The Spirit is here spoken of in irreducibly emotional
> and experiential terms. For Paul the Spirit is the
> power of God which integrates emotion, thought
> and conduct in a life-giving way. ... But it does so
> precisely as the Spirit of Christ, the Spirit who
> brings us to share in the same intimate sonship
> which Jesus enjoyed on earth.[12]

What happened to Jesus, the Son of God, happens to us
who have been adopted into the family of God. The Holy
Spirit descends upon us, facilitating the Father's touch of
love and helps us to hear our Father's voice of love.

Keep in mind that the Spirit's work of adoption in our
lives is the antithesis of the work of the spirit of fear
which leads to slavery. A spirit of fear may be produced
by the fear of failing to keep the rigid dictates of the law,
as was the obvious case with the Pharisees, or by the
demonic forces in opposition to our full freedom as God's
children. In either case it is the powerful realization of
God's love that can deliver us and secure us. I know that
in my own life my deep historical fears of failing were the

greatest obstacle to my experience of the Father's love.

Several months after my experience in the Jacuzzi in Oklahoma City, I attended a leadership retreat hosted by our church. At that stage in my pastoral ministry I was still a little insecure because the church I pastored was not very big. You may not realize it, but a common area of insecurity for many pastors is the size of their congregation. At this particular time, I was preparing to send out my Associate Pastor to plant a new church. Toward the end of the retreat I brought him forward to commission him. As I was praying for him a disturbing thought popped into my mind. Jim was a charismatic leader – perhaps people from my church would decide to go with him when he left. Perhaps a <u>lot</u> of people. I envisioned my church, rapidly shrinking, and saw myself as a pastoral failure, rejected by my peers, alone. As this terrible vision developed, I felt fear creep through my body. What began as a nagging little fear in the back of my mind soon merged with all the historical fears I had been suppressing and I found myself paralyzed.

At the pinnacle of my pain I felt the presence of the Lord surround me. The light of his nearness began to break through the swirling darkness of my fearful thoughts. The pain within me solidified like granite in defiance of the Spirit's presence, but the power of God increased dramatically and the chilling rock of emotional pain shattered.

With that freeing touch my mind cleared and my focus turned heavenward. Then I heard these words almost audibly impressed on my mind, "You are my son! I love you! And you can never fail in my sight!" When I heard those powerful fatherly words for the first time in my life I broke into tears and sobbed uncontrollably for nearly fifteen minutes. The Father gently spoke to me saying "I am taking all the pain for all the years." When my crying ended I felt greatly relieved, emptied of pain yet strangely filled with a warm presence, the presence of the Father's love. I had received the witness of his love. I knew I was his.

After forty years of pursuit I had come to fully experience a father's love. After seventeen years of seeking the Father's love as a Christian I had come into his heavenly embrace. It was a life-changing experience, similar to Matt's and the evangelist Finney's. My experiences of the Father's love since then have been less dramatic but usually follow the same pattern: the Holy Spirit comes and I feel the warmth of the Father's loving presence and hear him speak kind things to me. Usually I am moved to tears, and the fears of my life melt away, similar to Lynn's experience. And in between the emotional moments I rest in the assurance that my Father really does love me. Wherever you are in your experience of the Father's love you can always ask for more in the name of Jesus. Then the Spirit will descend on you to do the work He always does, bringing people into the presence of the heavenly Father and giving witness of his love. The pursuit of the Father's love is beautifully summed up by Martin Lloyd-Jones:

> The ultimate object of salvation is not merely to keep us from hell, not merely to deliver us from certain sins; it is that we may enjoy "adoption", and that we may become "the children of God" and "joint-heirs with Christ". The "summum bonum" is to "see God", and while in this life, to know God intimately as our Father, and to cry "Abba, Father". Have you ever known it? This is what is offered us in the Gospel of our Lord and Saviour Jesus Christ. God forbid that any of us should stop at any point short of it![13]

4

PRODIGAL PROBLEMS

"Here we are confronted with passionate, dramatic tensions; the wild, headlong, catastrophic fall of a man and his being graciously caught up at the last moment. Here we see the wrongheadedness of our life, the many wrong turnings, and here we also see the everlasting arms that hold us up through it all." – Helmut Thielicke

I would like to share three short stories with you. See if you can identify some common themes in them. Perhaps they might remind you of a very well known Bible story.

During a pastor's conference in England a Lutheran minister responded to an invitation to receive prayer for spiritual renewal. Unable to receive an experience of the Spirit's fullness he reacted angrily towards those praying for him. He later confessed to me that he was frustrated in ministry because he worked so hard and never seemed to be blessed with any success. He was angry at God and felt alienated by him. He found himself trying to fill his loneliness with pornography, but his emptiness remained.

When we probed the core issues of his life we discovered a deep father wound. His father was very demanding and abusive. He was constantly striving to earn a father's love and often trying to fill the void with some form of immorality. He prayed, asking forgiveness for his sin and forgiving his father. He was immediately delivered from his deep-seated anger and his heart began to be filled with the healing love of his heavenly Father. He returned to the conference and was able to receive freely.

ℋ

The couple that sat across from me in my office were young, attractive, devoted to the Lord and very much in trouble. With her head buried in her hands she tearfully confessed her adultery. He sat erect, his head turned toward her in disdain and anger. His only thought: "How could she do such a thing to me after I have been so good to her?" His only option, divorce. She acknowledged her guilt and pleaded for mercy. Her explanation was offered in the hope of reconciliation.

She loved her husband but never felt fully accepted by him. Because of her past life he often warned her about unfaithfulness, was very jealous and treated her like she just wasn't on the same spiritual level. She acknowledged his zeal for the Lord but shared that his continual absence in pursuing success as a Christian musician often left her feeling alone. This was the soil for her failure.

As he listened he began to see her failure in a different light – in the light of his own failure to love her unconditionally. Suddenly he was able to feel his wife's woundedness, and not just his own. He began to weep as he realized that he, too, had failed. It took great courage for him to acknowledge his mistakes because the fear of failure had driven him his entire life, especially in serving God.

Further conversation revealed that each one had father wounds and a void crying out for a father's love. This emptiness contributed to their current crisis. As we prayed together forgiveness was exchanged and both joined hands in receiving the Father's love. They left with hope.

ℒ

Six hundred people waited expectantly for the approaching ministry time during a Father Loves You Conference. What happened was extraordinary. After teaching about the Parable of the Prodigal Son, I gave an altar call to anyone in pastoral leadership who felt that they had become like the elder son in the story. Perhaps they were striving for success and as a result were pushing their people to perform. Surprisingly, the majority of leaders came forward to repent. I joined with them as we asked the Father to forgive us and fill us with his love. Tears of relief and healing flowed.

I will never forget what happened after that. I had also taught about the younger prodigal's problem: filling his life with immorality instead of his father's love. So I invited anyone struggling with some form of immorality to come forward. Having just witnessed the repentance of their leaders and sensing a merciful, compassionate environment they came forward. Four hundred of them! The love of the Father met them, forgiving them, cleansing them, delivering them and filling them. The pastors moved among their people, praying for them. It was a beautiful sight.

Did you identify the Bible story that in many ways parallels these three true-life stories? I guess I gave it away in the last example. It is the famous Parable of the Prodigal Son. In that parable, and our stories, we see the two basic problems people face when they lack a father's love in their lives. They end up drifting into immorality or religious striving in their attempts to find love. In each situation the experience of the Father's love is a critical factor in their restoration and ability to move forward. In fact, immorality and religious striving are blocks to the full experience of the Father's love, and therefore must be removed from our lives. Henri Nouwen's synopsis of the parable offers some insight:

> In the parable of the prodigal son (see Luke 15: 11–32), there are two sons: the younger son, who runs away from home to an alien country, and the older son, who stays home to do his duty. The younger son dissipates himself with alcohol and sex; the older son alienates himself by working hard and dutifully fulfilling all his obligations. Both are lost. Their father grieves over both, because with neither of them does he experience the intimacy he desires.
>
> Both lust and cold obedience can prevent us from being true children of God. Whether we are like the younger son or the older son, we have to come home to the place where we can rest in the embrace of God's unconditional love.[1]

In some ways the whole world can be seen in the story. Those who have not come to know God as Father through faith in Jesus Christ fall into two camps. One camp resembles the younger son living in rebellious, immoral and indulgent sin. The other camp puts on the outwardly respectable appearance of the great world religions and goes hard to work at earning the favor of God. Both are lost and need the forgiving and loving touch of the Father found through Jesus.

The parable can also portray life in the church. When a person has become a Christian but has not experienced the love of the Father he may find himself drifting into the position of one of the two sons outside the Father's house. In the search for a father's affectionate love a Christian may get involved in immorality or substance abuse like the younger son. Philip Yancey, in his book, *What's So Amazing About Grace,* points out that the church is not immune to these types of prodigal problems: "Christians profess 'family values,' but some studies show that they rent X-rated videos, divorce their spouses, and abuse their children at about the same rate as everybody else."[2] Some Christians take another route to find the same love. They go to work for it through religious effort. However, they still can't fill the void. Both sons in the story live outside the house, distant from their father and desperately in need of love. Even after years of knowing the Father's love I find that in moments of insecurity I am tempted to drift into one of these two positions. We will explore this in greater detail in the next chapter.

Looking for Love in all the Wrong Places

The lyrics of Country-western music often focus in on the real issues of life. The famous song, "Looking for Love in all the Wrong Places," succinctly states the issue for many prodigals in the world today. Many try to fill their need for love with the same things the younger son did; but as the prodigal discovered, not only do these things fail to fill the void, they distance us from the only one who can. We can better understand this prodigal movement by taking a closer look at the path of the younger son:

> "Not long after that, the younger son got together all he had, set off for a distant country and there squandered his wealth in wild living. After he had spent everything, there was a severe famine in that whole country, and he began to be in need. So he went and hired himself out to a citizen of that country, who sent him to his fields to feed pigs. He longed to fill his stomach with the pods that the pigs were eating, but no one gave him anything" (Luke 15:13–16).

Luke tells us that the younger son wasted his inheritance on a wild lifestyle – in a later verse it becomes clear that the majority of the money was spent on prostitutes. The son distances himself from his loving father and goes looking for love in the wrong place, the place of sexual immorality. This is a perfect portrait of a person who does not fully appreciate the love of God the Father and attempts to meet the need for intimacy according to the ways of the world. Many non-Christians live a life that looks like this. Not knowing the Father through faith in Jesus they find themselves looking for love through sexual fulfillment, often in activities that the Bible says are immoral such as pre-marital sex, adultery, lustful pornography and homosexuality. These activities have certainly increased over my lifetime and seem to have gained acceptance as somewhat normal behavior in our society. Anyone who watches television, goes to many movies, reads popular magazines or takes a walk downtown in most of the major cities of the world knows that sex is being sold as the answer to the love needs of life. I was watching the news recently and heard that the most "hits" on an Internet website during a 24-hour period was 374,000. That website was a sexually explicit adult program. Monitored on that same day, the highest-hit non-sexually related website was only hit 37,000 times. What does that tell us about the times in which we live? There is a great hunger in our society for love, and there is a great multitude of prodigals looking in the wrong place to find it.

Sexual immorality is a counterfeit to the experience of the Father's love. In our childhood we needed the intimate, affectionate touch of our natural father's love to secure our deepest being. If we did not experience that we sorely need the healing touch of our heavenly Father's affectionate *philia* love. In our vulnerability the powers of darkness will offer to us a false affection in some form of immorality. Impure thoughts, pornographic viewing, lustful gazes, promiscuous encounters, adulterous affairs and homosexuality have this in common: they all offer an approximation of intimacy, where there is a warm emotional and physical feeling of affection. While God did design sex to provide intimacy and affection in the marriage relationship, in these illegitimate forms sex becomes a short-lived stimulant to our sense of being loved. But, as the Prodigal story makes clear, anyone who trusts in this for fulfillment ends up empty and starved for true love. When a Christian finds himself caught up in some form of immorality it betrays the fact that he is filling the void in his life with something other than the Father's love.

Several years ago while teaching on this subject at a conference, I sensed that someone there was on the verge of an adulterous relationship. With some hesitation I shared this with the audience at the end of the session. I said that I would be available to talk to the person in private if they were interested. No one came up during the break; however, later that afternoon during the last session's ministry time a young man came up to me and whispered in my ear, "I am the one you were talking about."

Sitting off to the side of the room he told me his story: "Recently I married a divorced woman with four children. Although she is quite a bit older than me we had a close and emotionally satisfying relationship during our courtship. However, once we got married things changed. The challenge of taking care of the kids and becoming a family seemed to separate us emotionally and even sexually. I felt abandoned by her. After a while I began to develop a relationship with a woman my age at work who was always available to listen to my problems. One thing has led to another and I am supposed to meet her at a hotel this afternoon. Your word earlier seems to have stopped me in my tracks."

I shared with him that there might be a deeper issue at work in his life; perhaps he was looking for love in the wrong place. Because he felt abandoned by his wife he was now trying to find that emotional intimacy with another woman. Since he was willing to sin against God and his wife, I suspected his sense of abandonment must have a deeper source. It turned out that he had been abandoned by his father at birth. I suggested that the missing love of his father was being sought in the wrong place – the arms of another woman – and like the biblical prodigal he needed to run for the arms of his Father in heaven.

This idea made sense to him intellectually, but he was unable to grasp it on an emotional level until I asked him this question: "Do you love those four boys who now call you father?"

"Oh, yes!" he replied.

"How do think they would feel if you go through with this and break up their home?"

"They would feel abandoned," he said, tears forming in his eyes.

"The way you felt when your father abandoned you?"

He began to sob. I explained to him that what he was feeling toward his sons was very similar to what the Father felt toward him; he loved him and cared for the pain of his abandonment. With that realization his heart was flooded with the Father's love, and his tears began to wash away the pain of his own abandonment. He had found the love he was looking for and it was in the right place. This prodigal returned home in the nick of time. He never made that afternoon's appointment.

Sexual immorality wasn't the only aspect of the prodigal's fatherless living; substance abuse or addiction was another. The term "wild living" used by Luke has the connotation of unrestrained sensual indulgence that would include drunkenness. Excessive drinking, and the modern-day usage of illegal drugs, are other common ways of dealing with deeper emptiness in life, especially historic father wounds. They can anesthetize inner pain or create a false sense of well-being. The young person with a cold beer in hand feels the artificial intimacy of the crowd and all is well. As Henri Nouwen points out, the emptiness of addiction is strongly related to the need for the Father's love:

> "Addiction" might be the best word to explain the lostness that so deeply permeates contemporary society. Our addictions make us cling to what the world proclaims as the keys to self-fulfillment: accumulation of wealth and power; attainment of status and admiration; lavish consumption of food and drink, and sexual gratification without distinguishing between lust and love. These addictions create expectations that cannot but fail to satisfy our deepest needs. As long as we live within the world's delusions, our addictions condemn us to futile quests in "the distant country," leaving us to face an endless series of disillusionments while our sense of self remains unfulfilled. In these days of increasing addictions, we have wandered far away from our Father's home. The addicted life can aptly be designated a life lived in "a distant country." It is from there that our cry for deliverance rises up.
>
> I am the prodigal son every time I search for unconditional love where it cannot be found. Why do I keep ignoring the place of true love and persist in looking for it elsewhere?[3]

It is just at this point of realized emptiness and lostness that people turn to Christ for salvation. Unfortunately, that does not guarantee that they automatically find the Father and fill their deep need for his love. In fact, the church has many members that struggle with addictive behavior, particularly in sexual immorality and substance abuse. The deep voids in their lives, often caused by damaging relationships with their fathers, have never been filled by an experience of the Father's love. Until they have that experience they are vulnerable to succumbing to temptation in these areas. Substance abuse can provide a false sense of well-being and affection. It can also anesthetize our inner core of pain so that we do not have to face it.

Shane was a new Christian, married with children, a hard worker and a struggling alcoholic. His drinking kept him tied into the wrong crowd. This hindered his walk with the Lord and threatened his marriage. Fiercely independent, he refused any group help. He was determined to wrestle this demon himself. One defeat led to another.

Eventually, his pattern of drinking led to misconduct with another woman while under the influence, and the resulting crisis in his marriage brought him to my office. Counseling revealed that he had been abandoned at birth. His drinking dulled the deep pain of losing a father's love and the camaraderie of his drinking buddies helped fill the void. Unfortunately, his drunken state weakened his guard and he was tempted to further fill the void with illicit affection.

With this new understanding and out of total desperation he repented of his drunkenness, forgave his father and cried out for the Father's love. The Spirit came upon him powerfully, delivering him from the stronghold of alcoholism and adopting this long-abandoned son.

The Pathway Home

The parable of the prodigal not only shows us how we pursue the wrong things in search of love, it also shows us very clear steps to take to come home to the Father and receive his love. By taking these steps we can empty ourselves of things that are illegitimately occupying that emotional and spiritual space deep within us that is reserved for righteous love, particularly *philia* love from the Father. False loves block out the experience of the Father's love. We must empty ourselves of these in order to make room for the Father. Through the steps of *remembering, repenting* and *receiving,* the younger son, as well as those whose lives we have illustrated, emptied themselves of false loves and appropriated the fullness of the Father's love.

The first step the prodigal took was to remember what a loving father he had. Luke writes:

> "When he came to his senses, he said, 'How many
> of my father's hired men have food to spare, and

here I am starving to death! I will set out and go back to my father and say to him: Father, I have sinned against heaven and against you. I am no longer worthy to be called your son; make me like one of your hired men.' So he got up and went to his father" (Luke 15:17–20).

He came to his senses concerning his father. Either he had forgotten or never fully realized what a loving father he had. Suddenly his mind cleared and he knew the truth: that he needed the love that had eluded him in his worldly pursuits. Today the Holy Spirit comes to us to bring us to our senses concerning the Father and his love. He comes to remove our misconceptions of the Father caused by poor relationships with our natural fathers. At times he uses secular media to draw our attention to father issues in our lives. He comes to the church to remind us to include the Father and his love in our theology and experiential pursuit. He comes to the individual to remove lies that the evil one, the father of lies, has placed in our minds. He comes to help us see our core emptiness and the futility of false loves used to fill it. He comes again and again to tell us that our Father in heaven loves us. He comes to bring us to our senses. Only then can we truly take the next step, the step of repentance.

Repentance means to change our minds about something to the degree that our feet will follow. In other words, if we are headed in the wrong direction we do an about-face and do what is right. This is exactly what the young prodigal does: "'I will set out and go back to my father and say to him: Father I have sinned against heaven and against you.'" (Luke 15:18)

I call this "good repentance." He gets up, leaves his sin behind and goes home to his father. There he finds his father's compassionate love. Repentance opens us to the redeeming power of the blood of Jesus through which we find forgiveness and freedom from strongholds of sin. Whether it is sexual immorality, drunkenness, greed or any other prodigal sin we must turn from it if we are to fully experience the Father's love. It is interesting to note that what motivates the prodigal's repentance is his memory of his father's love and what culminates his repentance is the loving embrace of his father. Love could be called the bookends of healthy repentance. It is a better motivator than fear to change our ways; especially long-term. As Helmut Thielicke says in his book, *The Waiting Father,* "The repentance of the lost son is therefore not something merely negative. In the last analysis it is not merely disgust; it is above all homesickness; not just turning away from something, but turning back home."[4] And love culminates sincere repentance by cleansing, healing and filling our emptiness.

The beautiful centerpiece of the parable is the picture of

the prodigal receiving his father's love. Luke gives a vivid description: "So he got up and went to his father. But while he was still a long way off, his father saw him and was filled with compassion for him; he ran to his son, threw his arms around him and kissed him" (Luke 15:20). In his father's arms he finds what he has been searching for. He experiences the love of his father. His emptiness is filled. He is home.

This is a wonderful picture of how we experience the Father's love in our lives. Our Father in heaven is always watching us, even when we drift away from him. He waits for our return. And when we come back, eyes downcast, knowing we have failed him, he feels compassion for us. I think many of us anticipate condemnation and punishment whenever we fail, however, this story reveals the opposite. We are told that our Father actually feels compassion for us. His deep affection for us moves him to embrace us with forgiving and comforting love. Luke describes the father throwing his arms around the son and kissing him repeatedly. This is a portrait of the Father's love. It is exactly what *philia* love looks like – demonstrated natural affection. When we experience the Father's love in our lives we feel the embrace of his presence. The warmth of his affection touches our hearts. In our Father's arms we find our emptiness filled. We are home.

This moment of closure was experienced by each person whose prodigal story was told in this chapter: the Lutheran pastor, the troubled young couple, the hundreds of conference attendees struggling with immorality, the married man on the verge of an affair and Shane, who struggled with substance abuse. Each one traveled the path of the younger son and then returned home. There they found the waiting embrace of the Father. And in his arms they discovered the love they had been searching for their whole lives. Perhaps you can identify with their stories in some way. In our search for the Father's love, many of us will have to deal with problems similar to the ones they faced. Through the Parable of the Prodigal Son the path home to the Father's love has been revealed. Others have found their way home. If you are searching and have drifted from home I pray that you can find your way back now. The One who loves you is waiting for your return.

5

COMPETING
FOR LOVE

"This is and has been the Father's work from the beginning – to bring us into the home of his heart. This is our destiny." – George MacDonald

When Bob sat down in my office I couldn't help but notice that he was agitated. He really didn't want to be there, he told me, but he had to get something off his chest. He had visited our church the preceding Sunday because he heard that we prayed for the sick in our services. Bob suffered from severe cluster headaches. After the message he came forward for prayer. As he neared the front of the sanctuary he saw that some people were crying and trembling as they received prayer. "Emotionalism!" he thought. He noticed that women were praying for the people who came forward, and that in one situation a woman was praying for a man. "These women don't know their proper place in the church," he thought. And when he saw children mingling among the adults, "Out of order!" He stormed off angrily, put off by this disturbing scene. Now, days later, he had come to give me a piece of his mind.

After listening to his complaints I asked him if he was angry about anything else in his life. He thought for a moment, then told me he was pretty angry at God. This was his reason: "I have been a Christian for many years now and have worked very hard to please God. I read the Bible and pray every day. I pay my tithes regularly to the penny. I've got my wife and my kids in proper biblical order. I serve faithfully in my church. And what do I have to show for it? I'm tired, feel frustrated and have these lousy headaches that God evidently isn't going to do anything about. I obey him and he leads me to a place that is out of order and can't possibly help me."

I tried to explain to Bob that something was happening during the ministry time that he was failing to see; that God was making his merciful presence known to the people who needed healing. As he touched them deeply with his compassion, many people cried in relief. Women were praying because they had equal rights in the ministry of mercy. And who could bar the children from rushing forward as they saw their parents being touched by God's love? In fact, I explained, mercy was a higher priority for us than a rigid code of conduct. "Bob," I said, "you have been talking a lot about what you've been doing for God. What has God done for you lately?" His immediate response was, "Hell if I know!" Pardon the candor here, but this statement captures his emotional state. He was very frustrated and angry.

At a loss for words, I suggested we just ask God to be merciful to Bob that afternoon. I prayed and we silently waited. Suddenly Bob began to cry. He had just been surprised by a vivid memory from his childhood. He saw himself as a little boy sitting next to his father in the family car. His father pointed at a storefront sign, asking him to read it, but Bob stumbled through his attempt to sound out the letters. Tears welled up in his eyes as a deep frown of disapproval settled on his father's face. He looked up at me with those same tears in his eyes, saying, "No matter what I did, it was never good enough for my dad. I could never get him to tell me he loved me just the way I was!"

As Bob shared I found my eyes moistening as I remembered my own struggle to earn a father's love. I sensed that the Father in heaven was drawing close to Bob, touching him with his love right at the point of his pain. I explained that his relationship with his dad was a lens through which he viewed God, and that this lens gave him a distorted image of his heavenly Father. As a result he had been striving to earn love through his religious performance. It was time to forgive his father and reach out to receive mercy, compassion and love from his Father in heaven.

Bob prayed and the Spirit of the Father fell upon him. He burst into tears, and while trembling in the presence of God, cried out the pain of his rejection, his fears, his fatigue, his frustrations and the build-up of emotional pain that was the primary cause of his headaches. Bob was touched by mercy and his enslavement to religious works was over. He had come home to a Father who loved him for who he was and not for what he did.

Laboring for Love

Before he discovered the Father's love, Bob, like myself, bore some resemblance to the elder brother in the Parable of the Prodigal Son. We all worked hard for love. We became weary, frustrated and angry due to our failure to find love. We were critical of the people who didn't perform to our standards, and jealous of those who had the emotional experiences of love we desired. These characteristics also describe another group in the Bible: the Pharisees. In fact, this parable was given primarily for their benefit. Notice how Luke begins the chapter: "Now the tax collectors and 'sinners' were all gathering around to hear him. But the Pharisees and the teachers of the law muttered, 'This man welcomes sinners and eats with them'" (Luke 15:1–2).

Throughout his ministry, Jesus demonstrated the Father's merciful and compassionate love to sinners, people who had certainly not earned it through exemplary religious performance. The Pharisees believed that they earned God's favor through their own self-righteous works, and were threatened by a relationship with God based on mercy and grace alone. Thus they were very critical of Jesus and those sinners who responded to him. This story was meant to get their attention in the hope that they would change their ways. Whenever we read the parable we should pay close attention to the elder brother so that we may recognize any modern-day Pharisaism in ourselves and, like Bob, find our way home to our merciful and loving heavenly Father.

In the parable the older son is hard at work in the fields outside his father's house. When he heard of his wayward brother's return,

> "The older brother became angry and refused to go in. So his father went out and pleaded with him. But he answered his father, 'Look! All these years I've been slaving for you and never disobeyed your orders. Yet you never gave me even a young goat so

> I could celebrate with my friends. But when this
> son of yours who has squandered your property
> with prostitutes comes home, you kill the fattened
> calf for him!'" (Luke 15:28–30).

Here we see the major symptoms of what we might call "the elder brother syndrome." He has been slaving for his father in the fields. This portrays the *religious striving* Jesus was addressing in the Pharisees. He also has a *resentful attitude* toward his Father. He is angry because he feels all of his hard work has gone unrewarded. Finally, he demonstrates a very critical spirit toward his brother, who does not deserve such gracious treatment from everyone. These three symptoms require closer examination.

Religious striving could be defined as attempting to earn the love of God through good works. The Bible makes it clear that we gain a right status before God our Father through his grace, not our works. Once we become Christians, our good works should flow naturally out of our love for God. But often we find ourselves striving to get God to love us. Why do we do this? One reason is that it is our fallen human nature to attempt to achieve a right standing with God through our own effort. The other is that, even after becoming Christians, we have not truly come to know the Father or experience his unconditional love. Our insecurities drive us to perform for God, to try to earn the love we desire. In our ongoing search for love we venture outside the Father's house and go to work to earn God's love. In doing so we assume the position of the elder brother.

This is apparently what happened to the elder son in the story. He didn't comprehend the true nature of his father's love and thought he had to work hard to earn it. And the harder he worked the farther out in the field he got, increasingly distant from the love he grew more and more desperate to experience. This is the nature of true love: the harder we work for it the more it eludes us. That was the case with the Pharisees. In their attempts to faithfully observe the Law they drifted into self-righteousness and veered away from an intimate relationship with the Lord. The farther they drifted from God the more their hidden insecurities drove them to follow increasingly strict rules in a futile effort to earn his love. This was the position Bob found himself in. It's the same position I was in when I tried to "hit the glove" for God.

When we find ourselves striving for the Father's love we have assumed the position of competition. We are performing to get love. We compete within ourselves and with other people to be out in front in life, in that place where we believe God might see us and bestow his blessing on us. The elder son was in competition with his younger sibling and in his own eyes he was winning. The Pharisees competed with the Sadducees by observing a stricter code of religious conduct. Bob and I strove to stay far ahead of the average Christian in doing good works. We both thought we were winning and that we deserved the prize of love, but in fact we were just distancing ourselves from it.

In our society competition is a way of life. In the positive sense competition is the pursuit of excellence which finds its just rewards. Pursuing Olympic Gold is but one example. As Christians we are to pursue excellence in our service to God, but the deep insecurities that can exist in our personal and corporate lives may harness us to a negative form of competition. When this happens we can succumb to competing in our religious disciplines, family management, financial triumphs, church achievements and positions. Even pastors have to watch for that competitive spirit as they grow their churches. Often there are indicators – red warning lights on the dashboard of life – that tell us we have arrived at this place of negative competition. All of a sudden there will be a flash of resentment, a flash of harsh criticism toward those around us.

Several years ago I attended a prayer meeting with about 300 local pastors. It was held at Saddleback Community Church, a very large, well-known church in our area pastored by Rick Warren. Now there is a phenomenon that occurs whenever pastors meet: any insecurities in their lives rise to the surface when they encounter pastors of churches larger than theirs. Usually we keep these emotions carefully hidden under our pastoral demeanor but occasionally they seep out. During Rick's opening greetings, many eyes were scanning the room, trying to guess how many seats were in this large sanctuary. We all managed to keep our composure until Pastor Rick told us that this 3,000 seat facility was the fellowship hall, being used while the real sanctuary was under construction, and filled five times every weekend for church services. There was an audible gasp from the pastors in the audience. Insecurities were tapped.

When I returned to the office of my significantly smaller church I tried to gain control of my rising insecurity. I pulled out a fresh yellow legal pad and jotted down a few things I had noticed at Saddleback that we could implement for church growth. My pencil picked up speed as I thought of more and more ideas. As I was reaching a frenzied pace on the fourth page my secretary buzzed me: "Just wanted to remind you that you have an appointment with your dad in half an hour." I had promised to take him to the golf course driving range. My father, once an avid golfer, was now legally blind and could not drive himself there. I found myself resenting having to leave my church growth plans to spend several unproductive hours at the range, but as my attitude grew increasingly negative I began to realize what was going on. My insecurities had been stirred up at the pastors' meeting and I was caught in the elder brother syndrome. I was determined to work harder and build a bigger church that would make me feel better about myself, make me feel loved. As I headed out to pick up my dad, I tried to center myself again in the Father's love.

As I guided my dad to an empty practice mat I noticed the stylish clothes and expensive clubs of the other golfers. They all seemed to be staring at the three rusty clubs my dad had fished out of a golf course water hazard. I began to feel a little embarrassed. This was not helping my insecurities. I helped my dad line up at the tee, but his first swing missed the ball entirely and nearly decapitated the man next to us. His second attempt sent a ball buzzing through the grass, cutting a swath to the far right. I thought about how much I could be accomplishing at the church, and my frustration grew. I lined my dad up one more time, and he drew back the club and took a swing with perfect form. I heard the click of clean contact as the five-iron sent the ball in a beautiful arched trajectory over 180 yards. My dad looked up at me with his blurry vision to get my response. "Good shot, Dad!" I said, and my frustration melted as we made eye contact. For a moment I thought I saw a tear in his eye. I know there were several in mine. Through this moment of love between me and my dad I felt my heavenly Father's love touching me. My resentment was gone. I was centered again. I could measure the success of my life by the Father's love for me and my love for one person, not the size of my church. The elder brother syndrome was broken.

Resentment is often a warning that we have begun to strive to earn love. It comes from the frustration of not experiencing the love we are working so hard for. Resentment can also be the result of fatherlessness in our lives. The lack of a father's love in our childhood produces a painful, undeserved wound. The natural response to this is anger, and anger often turns into deep-seated resentment because young children are unable to process and heal such wounds through forgiveness. Ongoing attempts to earn a father's love only add to the well of resentment. The combination of our childhood resentments with the frustrations of adult religious striving can leave an angry edge on our lives. This angry edge is an indicator that we need the Father's love to heal our woundedness and free us from our striving.

Emerging out of the combination of competitive striving and growing resentment is a critical spirit toward others. The elder son was critical of his brother. The Pharisees were critical of the tax collectors and prostitutes, Bob of the "emotional" people at church. A critical spirit declares that others have not worked as hard as we have and therefore do not deserve to be blessed as much as we do, let alone more. A critical spirit is the natural by-product of a competitive attitude, which says that we must win in order to be loved. We want to see others as less capable or less deserving than ourselves. When the prodigal got the party, the calf and the best robe, it caused the elder brother to bring out the big guns of criticism to try to re-establish his priority. Whenever we find ourselves jealous and judgmental toward others we probably need to take a good look at where we are coming from ourselves.

From time to time I find myself in that critical place toward an individual or group of people, and I have to examine my heart to see if I have drifted out of the Father's house again. Several years ago I was on an aeroplane returning from a very successful conference on the Father's love. Filled with energy overflowing from the meetings, I began to work zealously on upcoming projects in my home church. Somehow I slipped into the old "hit the glove" mentality without being aware of it. I discovered the drift too late. As I pulled into my driveway at home I pressed the button for the automatic garage door opener and parked the car. Two things caught my attention almost simultaneously: my wife coming out to greet me, and a very large pile of laundry lying on the garage floor in front of the washer. My first words to her as she threw her arms around me were, "What have you been doing while I was gone?" Those foolish and fatal words escaped from my mouth before I really thought them through. They revealed the state of my heart, which was in the grip of the "elder brother syndrome." Janet immediately backed away, pinched her upturned nose and said, "My, aren't we religious!" Caught! Outside the house. Competitive. Critical. Fortunately, my wife showed compassion to me and let me in. Of course, that was after some good repentance.

Coming in from the Fields

Coming in from the fields is a challenging process that requires God's help. The elder son does not return to his father's house easily. In fact, the parable closes with him outside. The Pharisees did not readily respond to Jesus. With a few exceptions (Nicodemus and Joseph of Arimathea), they just couldn't leave their religious ways. It was a hard road that Bob traveled when he came out of the fields and returned to the Father. I labored for eighteen years as a Christian before finally finding the Father's love. Over the years I have observed the difficulty many "elder brothers" have had in seeing the futility of striving and recognizing their real need for the Father's love. But I have also seen that the Father does not give up on us when we are in that position. He reaches out to invite us, intervene in our lives, lead us to repentance, and fill us with his love.

One of the most amazing moments in the story is when the father leaves the party, goes outside and invites the older son to come in and join the celebration. The son is angry at his father, and accuses him of unfairness. In his anger, he doesn't recognize the loving care the father has given to both of his sons. But the father remains in a loving posture, despite his son's resentment. This is a beautiful picture of how the Father treats his children. When we strive for love and drift outside the Father's house, his love compels him to come and invite us back. He must come to us because in the midst of all our hard work we don't see that we are really lost and need help. Henri Nouwen helps us identify this dilemma:

> The lostness of the elder son, however, is much harder to identify. After all, he did all the right things. He was obedient, dutiful, law-abiding, and hardworking. People respected him, admired him, praised him, and likely considered him a model son. Outwardly, the elder son was faultless. But when confronted by his father's joy at the return of his younger brother, a dark power erupts in him and boils to the surface. Suddenly, there becomes glaringly visible a resentful, proud, unkind, selfish person, one that had remained deeply hidden, even though it had been growing stronger and more powerful over the years. ... The lostness of the

resentful "saint" is so hard to reach precisely because it is so closely wedded to the desire to be good and virtuous.[1]

The elder brother could not see the sin in his arrogance, resentment and condemnation toward both his father and brother. Drunkenness and prostitution are easier to see and turn from. Self-righteousness is a more difficult sin to recognize in ourselves. But our Father does not give up on us. He comes looking for us and lovingly helps us get in touch with our real condition.

Jesus was a messenger from the Father inviting the religious brothers to respond to love and come home. Some of his harsh words to them were last-ditch efforts to put them in touch with the error of their ways so that they might repent and return to the Father. Today the Father often sends others to come out to us in the fields and offer the invitation to come home.

God used John Wimber as a spiritual father to extend his invitation of love to me. When I first met John I was in the midst of a crisis – leaving my first pastorate after a serious difference of opinion with the governing church board. I was very vulnerable to feelings of failure, and found myself striving to prove myself as a pastor worthy of John's friendship. After several years of hard work I didn't feel my performance adequate. However, at that very time my wife and I received an invitation to John's fiftieth birthday party. While I was thrilled to be invited, I was extremely anxious at the prospect of being around John's deserving friends with larger churches.

On the way to the party I grumbled at my wife for forcing me to go. Remarkably, John and the other guests reached out and welcomed me, and I had a great time. On the way home I was deeply perplexed over how John and his friends had treated me. I asked my wife, "Why did John invite me? I don't have a big church like the rest of his friends at the party. Why me?" Janet answered with words I will never forget: "Maybe it's because he loves you." I began to weep. I suddenly became aware that I was loved not for what I did but for who I was. I believe that at that point I received the invitation to come home. In the years after that incident I followed John closely. He led me out of the fields and into the Father's house.

When invitation is not enough to get our attention God sometimes acts in another way. I call it intervention. The Father intervenes by allowing crises to occur in our lives that cause our carefully constructed world of good works to fall apart. We quickly get in touch with our inadequacies, insecurities and need for a love that is not based on our own efforts. His desire is that when things fall apart we will end up falling into his waiting arms of love. Troubles occurring in the areas of finances, marriage, ministry and health can effectively dismantle the prideful self-sufficiency of the elder brother.

Intervention came to Bob in the form of cluster headaches that could not be ignored. They forced him to stop his hard work. The moment he stopped working his underlying fears surfaced, demanding real attention. At that point Bob had his first experience of the Father's love. It would not be the last. In order to dismantle his strong pattern of performing for love, he would need other interventions. Each one led to a deeper infilling of love, until the pattern was broken.

When the Father's invitation to come home catches us outside the house it requires a change in us, a change of mind and direction brought about through repentance. This process begins with a realization that we have a wrong view of the Father's nature. We see him as harsh and demanding with little mercy or compassion. This is a false image that we must turn away from. We have to recognize that the "works mentality" has produced pride, self-righteousness and competition in us. These are products of our fallen human nature and must be repented of. It is helpful to remember that the resentment we deal with when we are in the futile striving mode may gain additional fuel from past wounds we have received and have not fully dealt with. This is especially true with long-standing, unresolved father issues. When we are critical, jealous or judgmental of others in our lives, we are often slipping back into elder brother syndrome. Repentance starts with a real awareness of these evils and a desire to change. This was a challenge to the elder brother in the parable. Fortunately, Bob and myself were awakened to our need and earnestly desired to change. That helped us move on to the next step: forgiveness.

Central to repentance is confessing our sins to our Father in heaven. We come to Him who loves us and tell him we are sorry for believing lies about his true nature. We tell him we are sorry for our prideful works and self-righteousness. We bring our sins of resentment, anger, jealousy and critical spirit to him to receive forgiveness for them. And forgiveness we find through the blood of Jesus shed for us. We receive cleansing and freedom from our guilt. An important part of this forgiveness is that we sincerely forsake these attitudes and actions in our lives. When we do so the power of Jesus' work on the cross sets us free from the stronghold of these sins so that we are fully released to return home to the Father's house and dwell in his love.

In our homecoming we find our Father with loving arms extended to embrace us. There the Holy Spirit fills our hearts with the Father's love. There we can rest in his love for us and find relief from all our striving. We can center our lives again on being loved for who we are, not for what we do. As we receive compassion we no longer have to compete for love. Back in the Father's house we look around and see others who were drawn there because of his compassion. We sense that we are one and can rejoice with all those who have come home to the Father through Jesus. We are no longer working in the fields. We are home, and everything looks different from this perspective. The Father's love does that.

6

FATHER ISSUES

"I have difficulty praying the Lord's Prayer because whenever I say, 'Our Father,' I think of my own father who was hard, unyielding and relentless. I cannot help but think of God that way." – Martin Luther

In the fall of 1992 my wife, Janet, was sitting in a hospital room alongside her father who was dying of cancer. After asking everyone to clear the room he drew her close, placed his aged hand on her head and pronounced a blessing of love and hope over her. Tearful, yet filled with joy, she left the room. Just days later her dad went home to be with the Lord. Suddenly Janet was helping her mother make funeral arrangements, visiting cemeteries to select grave-sites. Although she had wonderful closure with her dad, these activities put her in touch with his absence and her mother's aloneness, and unresolved emotions from her childhood began to surface.

Over the years Janet has shared many fond memories of her dad. He was an excellent pianist who gathered the family around the piano on holidays to sing together. He was a vibrant personality, often the life of the party. His theatrical ways were demonstrated to his children through delightful stories he made up about Sam and George, two mythical cats he corresponded with by mail. He often read their letters at the dinner table. Janet loved this fun and creative side of her dad. However, there was another side that had a negative impact on her life. During her early childhood, Janet's father was an alcoholic. He worked late into the night playing piano in restaurant lounges, and his frequent absences coupled with his alcoholism left her with deep feelings of emotional abandonment. When her father died, Janet felt those same feelings all over again.

Several weeks later Janet and I escaped to the seaside village of La Jolla, California to rest and share a romantic get-away. As it turned out, the Lord had other plans. During the first evening I became absorbed in my own thoughts and emotions and didn't pay attention to Janet's need for relational support. The next morning at breakfast she brought this to my attention in a round-about way: "Eddie, if you really cared for me you would have fixed the broken garage door opener so I wouldn't have to get out of the car and lift that heavy door all by myself!"

She went on to list other things I had neglected to take care of, growing more and more upset until finally she got up and stormed back to the hotel. I reluctantly followed.

As soon as I arrived she started up again, telling me it was time to increase our life insurance and secure our grave sites as soon as possible. After all, if I died she did not want be left to make painful arrangements and struggle with financial security all alone. I could tell that something deeper was troubling her. I agreed that we needed to look into these issues, but reminded her that if something happened to me she had a loving Father in heaven who would never abandon her and would always provide for her. Just then she burst out, "How do I know that he will be there for me when I really need him? You'll all die and leave me and I will be all alone in the end!" With that, the lonely little girl in her broke into tears. I reminded her that her heavenly Father was not like her dad in that way and that now was the time to forgive and release her father. This was her time to meet the Father in the fullness of his love. She agreed, and as she prayed the Father poured his love into the deep, empty recesses of her heart. She cried bittersweet tears as pain was removed and tender affection received. Her dad had gone home to heaven and her heavenly Father had come to make his home in her heart.

Broken Images

Janet could certainly identify with Martin Luther's words at the beginning of this chapter in that she viewed God as Father through the lens of her relationship with her natural father. Michael Phillips, in his book, *A God To Call Father*, identifies this perceptual problem:

> The common fallacy is to equate the fatherhood of one's earthly father with an accurate representation of God's heavenly Fatherhood. Though not intentionally, or even consciously, we draw this equal sign in our mistaken equation at a deep subconscious level very, very early in life.[1]

Our first perceptions of what a father is like come from observances of our earthly fathers. These perceptions are formed early in our childhood development and as a result are deeply implanted in our minds. Now, I believe that God designed it this way. He gave earthly fathers his name as Father, and they were supposed to give their children an accurate picture of what a father should be. This would prepare them to understand God's Fatherhood as they grew up. However, sin came into the mix and messed it all up. Phillips comments on this:

> He created earthly fathers primarily to offer a picture of what he is like. Fathers, however, don't do a

very good job of showing us God's nature. …

    If earthly fathers are intended to be mirrors, reflecting back some image of God, there is no denying they are cracked and broken. The image they reflect is incomplete or distorted.[2]

Deeply embedded broken images of fatherhood present some of the most serious barriers to the knowledge and experience of the Father's love. As you read through earlier chapters of this book, you probably noticed that working through problems with an earthly father is part of each personal story of discovering the Father's love. I thought my heavenly Father demanded that I "hit the glove," just as my dad did. Janet feared that the Father would abandon her as her dad had. All of us will deal with this "father issue" to some degree on our journey to finding the Father's love in our lives.

    In Luke 11:11–13, Jesus acknowledged this very issue:

"Which of you fathers, if your son asks for a fish, will give him a snake instead? Or if he asks for an egg, will give him a scorpion? If you then, though you are evil, know how to give good gifts to your children, how much more will your Father in heaven give the Holy Spirit to those who ask him!"

Jesus is trying to convince his disciples that their Father in heaven loves them and wants to give good gifts to his children when they pray to him (cf. vs. 2–4). He uses the goodness that would normally be seen in caring earthly fathers as a lens, so to speak, through which to see the even greater goodness of the Heavenly Father. Jesus identifies the same perceptual grid of fatherhood that we have been discussing. He then points out the problem in this system: natural fathers are evil. The original Greek word used here suggests a malignancy that is injurious, and refers to the sinful condition of fallen man. In other words, human fatherhood is marred by sin. John Nolland calls it "flawed human fatherhood."[3]

It is important to realize that the father of lies, the devil, wants to use this flaw to his advantage. He doesn't want anyone to come to know the fullness of the Father's love. Through these natural father distortions he creates lies about the true nature of God the Father, especially his love. Phillips again:

> As in all things, sin interrupted and corrupted the process. The enemy has gone to great lengths to infiltrate the family unit, to discredit the earthly symbol of God's establishing. Instead of pointing us *to* God our Father, the incompleteness of earthly fatherhood has, with Satan's help, embittered sons and daughters *against* their parents and, in doing so, blinded them to the magnificence of God's Fatherhood.

Thus has been dulled, almost beyond recognition, the essential human instinct – that created yearning to look up and behold our Father. A gigantic stone sits in the middle of the road preventing each one of us from even thinking clearly on the subject, let alone getting past the obstacle.[4]

These "stones" are fortified by the enemy's power in such a way that they are more than just psychological misperceptions; they are spiritual strongholds that can only be removed by the power of God's Spirit. They stand in resistance to the experience of the Father's love and must be dismantled. However, before we can dismantle these obstacles, we must recognize them for what they are.

Common Distortions

Over the years I have found that father distortions fall into several general categories. This categorization may be a little simplistic as there are certainly exceptions and combinations of the categories that occur; however, they provide a helpful frame of reference.

The Performance-Oriented Father

The performance-oriented father gives love according to the performance of the child. Acceptance, affirmation and affection are attached to achievement in such areas as chores, education, sports, etc. Love is given or withdrawn in relation to the child's success. Performance demands can take a variety of forms: perhaps it is necessary to pursue a certain career, become a doctor or lawyer, to earn a father's recognition; perhaps a child must conform to a strict family dress code to be accepted with open arms. In a performance-oriented society this father-type is common. The proverbial carrot is dangled out ahead of the son or daughter, and this relational pattern often carries on into adulthood. Although there is a time and place for rewarding achievement, it should never be blurred with unconditional love and acceptance. Gordon Dalbey comments on this performance-oriented relationship in his book, *Father and Son:*

> Sadly, the average man today has learned legalism instead of mercy from his earthly father. "Do what I say and I will love you," he has essentially heard growing up; "disobey or make a mistake, and I will not love you." He has not seen his father model mercy either by forgiving his son's mistakes, or by asking the son to forgive him for his own mistakes. Thus the son grows up fearing failure, equating it with losing relationship with the father.[5]

The movie *Searching for Bobby Fischer* illustrates this concept powerfully. In it a young boy, Josh Waitzkin, is revealed to be a chess prodigy. His parents disagree over how to best encourage his talents. Josh's father pushes him to succeed in competition, fearing that his son's gift will be lost. His mother worries that more is at stake than Josh's success. Josh's performance in competition is increasingly inconsistent, as playing chess becomes less of a game and more of a means to win or lose his father's approval. In one powerful scene the parents, Fred (played by Joe Mantegna) and Bonnie (played by Joan Allen), have the following discussion:

> FRED: "If you're afraid to lose, you lose. If you lose you get more afraid. He's afraid."

> BONNIE: "He's not afraid of losing. He's afraid of losing your love. How many ball players grow up afraid of losing their father's love every time they come up to the plate?"

> FRED: "All of them."

A Christian with this type of father perceives his Father in heaven as one who requires a good performance in order to give the reward of love. A deep fear of failure often drives him into religious striving. This father-type is closest to my own experience, because I believed that I had to not only "hit the glove" for my dad but also for God the Father. Bob's story in the previous chapter also illustrates this category.

The Passive Father

The passive father does not actively demonstrate love to his child. He does not speak words of love, nor offer an affectionate physical touch of love. As a result the developing child is deprived of the emotional nourishment that demonstrated affection brings. Fathers in this category were either not home much, not emotionally open and available when they were home, or they simply never demonstrated love. Fathers who traveled constantly, were workaholics, alcoholics or emotionally stoic fit into this category. Alcoholics are mentioned here because they are often very self-absorbed, unable to give emotional support to others, including their children. Fathers can also be separated from their children through divorce or death. In such cases the child's need for a father cannot be met, because the father is simply not there. The resultant perception of God the Father is that he is distant, uninvolved, and undemonstrative. People with passive fathers often have difficulty getting in touch with their emotions and experiencing a tangible touch of the Father's love.

One of the principle problems a father's passivity produces in a child is a sense of abandonment. Physical or emotional abandonment causes the young child to feel alone. Being alone, separated from a father's love, is a painful experience. The resulting wound is usually deep and often difficult to get in touch with. A father's angry slap to the face produces a sharp pain that resides close to the surface. A father's silence produces a dull wound; equally painful, but harder to identify. It was easier for me to get in touch with the pain of my dad's rejection when I was losing the big game than it was for Janet to isolate the pain of her father's just not being there.

Abandonment can also produce a false sense of guilt in children. They blame themselves for their father's absence, believing they must have done something to make him stay away. They conclude that their father's failure to express love is their fault. As they grow up these children often go around collecting "guilt stamps," believing that everything that goes wrong in life is their fault. This compounds their difficulty of experiencing the Father's love. They believe not only that God is distant, but that he sees them with some kind of disqualifying black spot on their lives. Anger over the unfairness of it all builds over time, and often an explosion of emotions reveals this latent father issue, allowing healing to begin. Janet's deliverance started at the breakfast table in La Jolla.

The Punitive Father

The punitive father gives some form of abusive pain instead of love. This may take place through verbal, physical or sexual abuse. Abuse of this severe nature usually accompanies one of the father dysfunctions we have already addressed, and goes further to inflict deliberate pain. This breaks down the developing child and distorts any remaining image of healthy fatherhood. The healing of this brokenness and restoration of a correct father perception can be a challenging and complex process. Victims of abuse often perceive the Father as stern, harsh, punitive, unforgiving and certainly unloving. Fear, shame and anger are common emotional strongholds. These broken people desperately need the tenderness of the Father's love to enfold their fragile lives.

A man named Dave exemplifies this brokenness. When we met he was seeking counsel on whether it was wrong or right for him as a Christian to purchase a life insurance policy. I told him that God was probably neutral on the subject and it was really his choice. He quickly corrected me, saying that God would surely judge him if he made the wrong choice. In fact, he believed that he was currently experiencing an internal bleeding problem in his body because he had failed to live up to God's holy requirements in his life. I asked him where he had picked up such a fearful concept of his Father in heaven. He described his previous involvement with a very legalistic group of Christians. Then I asked him to tell me about his relationship with his father.

As a young boy he loved to spend time in the workshop where his dad made fine wooden furniture. Longing to be like his father, he accepted small assignments like shaping a piece of wood on one of the machines. But when his father came to inspect the finished product and found even the smallest flaw, he hit him with the wood on the side of his head. He told Dave that this wood was very expensive and that he better not make any more wasteful mistakes. Now I understood where this image of a punitive God was birthed.

After discussing how his relationship with his earthly father had distorted his image of God the Father, we prayed. Dave repented of believing a lie about God's true nature and then forgave his dad for the abusive treatment. After I blessed his prayer the Spirit of the Father fell on him. He shook as he was delivered from the spirit of fear that had gripped him all those years. He then looked up and told me he saw a picture in his mind of himself as that little boy, now climbing up on the lap of his heavenly Father, who gently caressed the side of his head where he had received so many painful blows. He wept tears of healing as he found a Father's love. Remarkably, the bleeding condition in his body disappeared.

The Pretty Good Father

In the last several years I have added this category to the father-types because there are those whose fathers were generally loving to them. Most fathers have good qualities mixed in with less desirable ones. Positive qualities have a good effect on the development of children and their God-images. This category looks at those fathers whose good effect far outweighed the bad. Keep in mind that there are no perfect fathers due to original sin. Everyone may have to deal with some distortion, however slight. I have observed that those with healthy father relationships usually have an easier time understanding and appropriating the love of the Father. There is, however, an interesting challenge that they face. They have to move beyond a good relationship with their earthly fathers and, in the spiritual sense, give themselves to their Father in heaven, trusting fully in Him for their deepest source of love. The best thing a father can do is to love his children and then introduce them to the Father in heaven, who can give to them a love that surpasses his own. Tri Robinson, a friend of mine who is a pastor in Boise, Idaho, has seen this principle worked out in his life:

> As a young boy growing up in the country, my fondest memories were of deer and quail hunting with my father. He was a great dad who had a deep conviction that if you took your boy hunting, you wouldn't have to hunt for your boy. He was a Christian and consistently took me to the Presbyterian church each Sunday, except during the peak of hunting season.

I always loved my dad and wanted to be just like him when I grew up. I so admired him that when I was too young to carry a gun, I would follow him and attempt to step in his footprints. When I was about twelve years old, I began to carry an old Winchester rifle that my dad had used some 25 or 30 years earlier to shoot his first deer. It was a great honor and a symbol of the independence and responsibility of manhood to me.

As a young boy I always called my dad "Daddy." At about 10 years of age I tried to train myself to refer to him as "Dad," especially in the presence of his friends and mine. Men who carry rifles call their fathers "Dad"– anyone knows that! With the change in titles also comes a change of perspective and atti- tudes. You can run to your daddy for security, but when you have a dad, you are an adult in behavior and a bit independent and cool.

One day when we were hunting the rolling hills of junipers together, my dad suggested that we split up and hunt separate ravines with the intention of meeting at a determined landmark. I'd never been alone in those hills before, but because I was now an official hunter, I couldn't refuse. We had been separated for nearly half an hour when I realized I wasn't sure where I was supposed to be, and I became increasingly anxious about it. Anxiety soon turned to fear and I began to cry out "Daddy" as loud as I could. This went on for what seemed like hours, but in reality it was probably only minutes. Suddenly, on a distant ridge I saw movement and I realized it was my father. I know he must have heard me, and I later realized he hadn't ever lost sight of me, but he never let on he'd seen or heard my panic. He just kept moving up that ridge in plain sight, making sure I was aware of his presence. All the fear and anxiety left me and I gave him a casual wave, yelling "Hey, Dad," in a voice just a few octaves lower.

Years later I found myself lost again. I wasn't lost from my earthly father, but from a heavenly Father who, like my natural father, had never lost sight of me, even in my aimless wandering. I'd been walking through life trying to be in control and "manly." I was independent and somewhat aloof from God, standing on my own two feet and bearing all the symbols of manhood. I had a good job, a frustrated but wonderful wife, and two young children. We had a great home in the country, horses, and an old dog named Blue. People saw me as a self-made man with a perfect life.

In 1979 my marriage hit a crisis and in the midst of it I became helpless and desperate. No matter how hard I tried, I couldn't seem to hold it together. I remember one Sunday afternoon when an argument escalated into war. A cup of coffee was thrown through a window and I snapped into a runaway rage. I lost my grip emotionally on anything sane or normal and began to tear the house apart. First chairs, then whole beds were turned over. I was out of control when all of a sudden my eyes connected with my then three-year-old son, who was staring at me in unbelief.

I can't explain it exactly, but his look at me as his "Daddy" triggered something very deep in me, something so deep I didn't even know it was there. I began to weep from deep within; I compulsively wept until I hurt. Years and years of issues, frustration, and pain from a life of independence from God the Father all came to the surface at once. Both my son and wife held onto me, and Nancy began to pray for God's intervention. She prayed that I wouldn't lose my mind, but that together we'd come into the fullness of the Father. I cried out that day to my "Abba Father." I chose to cling to Him in intimacy and brokenness; no longer to be aloof and independent, but open to His love for me.

I was again like that kid trying to find his way through the juniper hills, crying "Daddy" from the depths of my fear and insecurity. But this time when I was found, I just kept crying "Abba Father." I knew that He had never lost sight of me, but had just been waiting for me to see my need for Him.

Addressing Father Issues

I was 38 years old when I first began to address the father issues in my life. I had been a Christian for nearly sixteen years. Why did it take so long? I believe it was because the pain was so deeply embedded in me. Those faulty lenses were placed on my eyes very early on. Often we deal with most everything else before we finally confront this foundational issue. When we make an effort to correct the father issues in our lives, we enter a process of removing the broken lenses in order to see the Father as he truly is. Only then can we receive deep healing for the father wound through the Father's love and reconcile ourselves with our natural fathers. I have been involved in this process for several years.

To remove broken lenses we begin by identifying them and acknowledging their existence. Identification reveals the areas where a natural father failed to represent God's true nature. Fathers are responsible for their stewardship. To misrepresent God is to sin against their children. This is important to grasp because it is only through forgiving our fathers of these sins that we can remove the faulty lenses. Acknowledging the failures of our fathers can be difficult because we have strong denial mechanisms within ourselves. Recognizing that a father failed us makes us come face to face with the imperfections of his love. Allowing ourselves to feel unloved by our fathers to any degree is an experience we will usually avoid at all costs.

But removal requires forgiveness. We must forgive our fathers for their sins against us, and we do this primarily through prayer. We come to our heavenly Father and forgive our earthly fathers in Jesus' name. In prayer we bring the distorted lenses we wear and the painful wounds of our past into the presence of our eternal Father, who is not limited by time. As we forgive our fathers for the past, our Father reaches down and takes the distorted glasses from our eyes so that we can see him clearly. He touches the pain of our childhood that is frozen in time past and heals our woundedness. Some of us may even have the opportunity to reconcile with our fathers face to face.

At this point it seems appropriate to issue a few words of caution: forgiving our fathers should not be confused with blaming our fathers. We can't hold them responsible for every difficulty that we have experienced since childhood. Even though we may have been injured by them, we are responsible for our reactions to them and the choices we made in our attempts to find love and happiness in our lives. For example, a young man cannot blame his abusive father for his choices to find happiness through a lifestyle of substance abuse. He must forgive his father for wounding him but take personal responsibility to seek God for forgiveness, healing and deliverance from his own sin. Forgiving our fathers should not be confused with dishonoring our fathers. The Bible makes it abundantly clear that children are to honor their fathers and mothers (Exodus 20:12, Ephesians 6:2–3). We can maintain a posture of respect and love toward our fathers while we work through these issues with God. This calls for great sensitivity and care in our speech concerning our fathers. To deal with these issues, leaving behind our bitterness and estrangement and moving toward reconciliation with our fathers, is indeed the action of honoring the God-given relationship.

Forgiving our fathers frees us from bitterness and broken images of fatherhood, but it releases us in other ways as well. We no longer have to wait for our fathers to come to us and right the wrongs of the past. It often seems as if we are still little children, standing there waiting for our fathers to come and tell us that they love us or tell us they are sorry. In many situations this never happens, and as a result we are frozen in our childish state and unable to move on. Releasing our fathers in prayer frees us to get on with our lives. It also allows us to break away from focusing on them in an unhealthy way. Protracted focus on our fathers for negative treatment can sometimes cause the same negative characteristics to form in our lives. Forgiveness helps release us from walking in the sins of our fathers. Unforgiveness can connect us in a negative spiritual way to our fathers, and the sins they struggled with can then slide down the connecting line and dominate our lives. At times the father's sins of drunkenness, immorality, or child abuse are passed down from generation to generation, traveling along lines of bitterness, unforgiveness and judgment. Forgiveness cuts down the lines and sets us free.

Flowing out of forgiveness and release is the potential for reconciliation with our natural fathers. Reconciliation can take the form of proper closure with a father who has passed away or cannot be located. It most often takes place in establishing a new relationship with our living father. Working through the issues of forgiveness and release with God before we attempt this earthly reconciliation is very important. Having received compassion, we are in a better place to give it. Having worked through our childhood pain and perceptions, we can better relate to our fathers in an adult-adult exchange. We are also able to maintain some protective boundaries if our fathers are still in a place to hurt us. Henri Nouwen takes note of this in his book, *Sabbatical Journey:*

> I talked to my father today by phone. I asked him, "What do you think of my daily column in the Dutch newspaper?" He paused and said carefully, "Some are better than others. … It is not easy to write a column." Although his response was not very different from his responses to my high school performances, and quite in character, I still felt a little hurt.[6]

Often, when we've worked through the negative aspects of our father relationship, we can appreciate positive qualities that we were blinded to before. The father who was never home may have been working hard to make sure there were presents under the Christmas tree. Even though his distance hurt, knowing that he was dedicated to helping us enjoy life helps us to appreciate him more.

When I became a Christian, things began to change in my relationship with my dad. I was embarking on a long road to reconciliation. Years later, after seeing God change my life, he ventured to our church for an evening communion service. There I had the privilege of praying with him to receive Jesus into his heart. Our relationship took on a new spiritual dynamic. Over the following years there were times of acknowledging each other's faults and expressing forgiveness. As I began to discover the Father's love in my life I realized that I had to deal with even deeper issues with my dad. I came to understand how much I had longed to hear the words, "My son, I love you!" Though my father and I were closer than ever, he still had never said those words to me.

One morning early in 1987, I received word that something was wrong with my dad. He asked me to come quickly. When I arrived I found that he had a severe attack of diverticulitis and was bleeding heavily from within. I immediately prayed for him. Miraculously, the bleeding stopped, and we then rushed him to the hospital. He had lost a lot of blood and required a transfusion. Later, I was sitting alongside him in the Intensive Care Unit. Just then he reached out to me. I took his hand and held it. He looked into my eyes and said, "You know, Eddie, I love you." I said, "Yes, and I love you." We both had tears in our eyes. Reconciled! That day the love was flowing from father to son and from son to father and from God the Father to his sons. The broken lenses were gone and we at long last could see through the eyes of love. Our relationship with each other and our Father in heaven has been growing richer ever since.

7

THE CHILDREN'S BREAD

"But the revelation of God in Jesus Christ is that we have a merciful Lord who saves and heals. Jesus, as the visible manifestation of the invisible God, shows us that God is a loving Father. ... that God really loves us; for the most tangible sign that God loves us is that he stoops, as Jesus did, to heal the wounded." – Francis MacNutt

When she first stepped out of the crowd of people coming forward for prayer, I could not hide a startled gasp. Her body was visibly crooked, with one shoulder dipped several inches lower than the other. She was responding to an invitation John Wimber had given for people with skeletal deformities to come and receive healing prayer. I was one of the prayer team accompanying John to this Healing conference in the city of Brighton, England. As she stepped forward I met her, and our team members interviewed her in order to determine how we should pray. She told us that the bones in her lower back and pelvic area had been malformed from birth. One leg was shorter than the other, resulting in the shoulder slump I had already noticed. We began to pray. We sensed the presence of the Lord, but no visible change was occurring. Perplexed, I asked the Lord to give us directions. Immediately the word "rejection" formed in my mind. I prayed accordingly, "Lord heal her of any rejection she has experienced in her life." She screamed and slumped to the floor. I realized we had touched a deep nerve of pain running through her life.

Kneeling beside her, I asked when she had experienced rejection, and she told us a story I will never forget: "When I was born I had a twin sister who was stillborn at the same time. I had skeletal formation problems but was otherwise healthy. These problems put a financial and emotional burden on my parents. When I was five years old, I was standing outside the kitchen and I heard my father say to my mother, 'I'll never understand it. Why did the one with the perfectly formed body die and the one with the deformities live?' I know my father was speaking out of his frustrations with the challenges of caring for me, but nevertheless it really hurt. I've never been able to forget it."

I explained the importance of forgiving her father for what he said as a step in the healing process. I told her that she had a Father in heaven who wanted to touch her with his love and heal this wound of rejection. So she prayed and forgave her father. We then prayed that the Father would come. An amazing thing happened.

Tears streamed down her face as the Father's love began to carry away the deep pain of rejection. But as she was crying I noticed that there was also movement in her body. I reached out and held her heel and prayed that the shortened leg would be healed. It moved! And as her cries of emotional relief deepened, her leg straightened out to its correct length. We asked the Father to pour his love into her whole life, and her bones responded with cracking sounds as the Creator of the world reshaped them. When he was done, she stood, face tear-stained and shoulders perfectly level. This daughter of God had received the children's bread, the healing that flows out of the Father's love.

The Healing Power of Love

"The children's bread" is a term Jesus used for the healing that comes from his Father in heaven (Matthew 15: 21–28). When a Gentile woman asked him to heal her demonized daughter, Jesus told her that the children's bread was first of all for the children of Israel who recognized God as their Father. Nevertheless, her ardent request stirred the compassion of Jesus and he healed her daughter. These verses remind us that our Father in heaven wants to provide healing for us just as naturally as a merciful and kind father would want to provide food for his family. In our pursuit of a deeper experience of the Father's love we find that our periodic need for healing opens a window for us to see even more of his loving activity in our lives. The knowledge of the Father's love for us increases our experience of healing in two ways: first, when we know the Father loves us we have more faith to believe he wants to heal us. Second, the experience of the Father's love is a dynamic catalyst for the release of healing in our lives, as occurred with the woman in England.

The awareness that the Father really loves us creates a receptivity to healing that comes from heaven above. Jesus taught that we are not to fear because the Father is pleased to give his kingdom to his children (Luke 12:32). When physical affliction comes our way we need to have confidence that the Father desires to send us healing from heaven because he loves us. Many people are unreceptive to healing because deep within they have doubts concerning the Father's love for them. They feel unworthy of receiving God's help in their lives. As they receive the good news that the Father loves them, they open up to the opportunity to be healed.

I first observed this dynamic while praying for people in a London church who were partially or completely blind. After praying for several people without much effectiveness, I stopped to evaluate the situation. There was obvious need and I sensed the powerful presence of the Lord there to heal, but little healing was taking place. I asked the next few people in line for prayer what they were anticipating God would do. Several believed that God was there to heal others, but were not so sure that they themselves were worthy of healing. I realized that many of the people I had met in England had distant relationships with their fathers, leaving them unsure if they were worthy of being loved and cared for. This seemed to influence their perception of the Father's willingness to give them a loving gift of healing. I decided to tell each person I prayed for that the Father loved them just as he loved his Son Jesus, and that fact alone made them worthy to receive healing.

The next woman in line had a noticeably disfigured eye in which she had lost her sight. She also confessed that she felt unworthy to be healed. When she heard the message of the Father's love, she began to cry, and her faith increased. As we prayed, the power of the Holy Spirit touched her so strongly that she fell back. We reached down to help her up, and as she stood she opened her eyes. The disfigurement in her eye was completely gone. She quickly covered her "good eye." To her amazement as well as mine, she could see. Her heart was opened to the Father's love and then her blind eye was opened to see.

Not only can an experience of the Father's love prepare someone to be more receptive to healing, it can actually be a dynamic catalyst in the healing process. Years ago I became aware of the potential connection between emotional problems and physical sickness through the writing of Francis MacNutt. He found that medical research links such diverse illnesses as ulcerative colitis and cancer to emotional root causes such as despair, chronic resentment and anger. In his book *Healing,* he comments:

> There is good evidence, then, that there is a very natural connection between much of our sickness and our spiritual and emotional health. For very human reasons we can see why physical sickness can symbolize a deeper sickness of the human person.[1]

The experience of the Father's love touches two critical areas of emotional health: it fills the painful void that produces fear, hopelessness and despair; and it motivates forgiveness toward those who have hurt us, setting us free from the poison of bitterness and resentment. When the power of the Holy Spirit flows through us and brings us the deep experience of the Father's love, it seems to carry off emotional pain and poisons, facilitating physical healing. This was true for the woman with the skeletal defect, and also for Bob, whose healing from cluster headaches was described in Chapter 5. Of course, not every physical problem has an emotional root cause or is always related to a historical father issue, but in many cases these are important factors to consider in the healing process.

The healing of emotions is an area where the Father's love can be of great benefit because adult emotional problems are often related to childhood difficulties and parental dysfunction in particular: central targets for the Father's love. Dr. W. Hugh Missildine connects the two in his classic book *Your Inner Child of the Past:*

> As a child psychiatrist who has had the opportunity to observe the inner feelings of both children and adults as they struggle with their problems, I have been in a unique position to see *in the adult* what has happened to the child he once was. I often observe, *in their very origins,* the development of troublemaking attitudes in the child. They are the child's way of dealing with the often unreasonable or excessive attitudes and demands of his parents, the all-important people in his life. I see the end result of these childhood reactions in the adult – loneliness, anxiety, sexual difficulties, depression, fears, marital discord and compulsive striving for success.[2]

I found Missildine helpful in analyzing the problematic relationship between childhood pain and adult emotional problems, but his secular self-help solutions fall short of the healing potential we have in the Holy Spirit.

In the best-selling Christian book *The Blessing*, authors Gary Smalley and John Trent address the same relationship between childhood and current emotional distress. They refer to a child's reception of unconditional love as receiving "the blessing" of the parents, and describe the emotionally painful effect of not receiving it:

> Few people see themselves as struggling with missing out on their family's blessing, but people around them see it. Whether it is reflected in an underlying sense of insecurity, or, more blatantly obvious, in an angry, hostile spirit, we can hide very little from those who know us well.[3]

They go on to illustrate how emotional healing can take place where there have been childhood problems. Notice how they focus on negative father issues being healed through a relationship with God as Father:

> Some people will never, in this life, hear words of love or acceptance from their parents, people like Helen …
>
> Helen was never secure in her relationship with her father. His anger had frozen within her heart a

sense of insecurity. Yet when Helen trusted Jesus Christ as her Lord and Savior, she found out that she had a source of blessing that would be with her each day of her life and beyond! Helen discovered verses ... that speak of how stable her heavenly Father is and how permanent her relationship is with Him. ...

The first thing Helen had to consider when she came home at night was what kind of mood her father would be in. One night it would be anger, the next indifference; and occasionally he could even be very nice. His vacillations kept her so off balance, it left her insecure and questioning herself. Now she had a relationship with a heavenly Father characterized by the words, "He is the same yesterday, today, and forever" (Heb. 13:8 NASB).[4]

The Blessing was very helpful in my own pilgrimage toward emotional healing. I began to realize that my deep fears of failure had something to do with my relationship with my father, and that I needed a better connection with the love of my heavenly Father. But I also discovered that I had to go beyond just a new theological awareness of the truth of the Father's love. I needed to be experientially touched by the Father's love through the ministry of the Holy Spirit. I have found that many conservative evangelical Christian authors, counselors and pastors accurately point towards the Father to find the love we need, but sometimes fail to emphasize the importance of the actual experience of love that the Spirit's work of adoption brings. Negative emotions such as fear, guilt and anger are real and can be very powerful. We need greater experiences of the power of love to receive significant healing. A man named Eric discovered this truth first-hand:

> I had a normal childhood free from any major traumas like divorce or abuse. As a family we went on vacations together, celebrated holidays, and did the normal things families do. As I was growing up, my dad and I did many activities together. However, I often perceived him as being angry. I was not sure if he was angry at me or at something else. I also perceived him as being depressed or discouraged with his life and how things were working out. Perhaps he felt overwhelmed with the responsibilities of supporting a family. I had the impression that he did not really want to spend any time with me. He only did so out of obligation because he was my father.
>
> As a child, I blamed myself for many of the things my father felt. I often felt ashamed and terribly afraid. I felt that something was wrong with me. I also got very depressed at times. In order to over-

come these feelings, I attempted to do everything perfectly, above and beyond what was normally required. However, my anxiety and shame would never leave, despite my success in the eyes of my peers and family. I needed comfort and unconditional acceptance, which I couldn't seem to find through my own efforts.

I became a Christian as a sophomore in college, but it wasn't until four years later that I experienced the tangible, physical love from God the Father that began to bring lifelong healing to me. At a church retreat, Pastor Ed taught us that God the Father wants to touch us with his love. We were instructed to raise our hands, posturing ourselves to receive, if we wanted to experience this touch. Ed started to pray. All at once I felt a rush of emotions, and I started to cry. I felt shame and fear and happiness and freedom all at the same time. I knew that the Father was taking the pain out of me. My body felt warm all over and I started to shake. I also felt a warm tingling on my head, neck and down my back. One man who was praying for me said, "You can't fail in God's eyes. You are his son." I started weeping. I had never cried so hard before. Another friend said, "Eric, you've started a new journey today. You will never be the same again."

During that experience I finally felt loved and accepted, and I didn't have to do anything!

Deliverance from Oppression

When Jesus ministered on earth he delivered those who were oppressed by the devil (Acts 10:38). Many people had physical afflictions caused by a demon, including blindness and muteness (Matthew 12:22), crippling of the back (Luke 13:10), and perhaps even the fever suffered by Peter's mother-in-law (Luke 4:38–39). Although not all affliction is of demonic origin, some is, and therefore necessitates deliverance. Interestingly, when Jesus used the term "the children's bread," it was in the context of a need for healing that required deliverance. Demons still exist today and most Christian leaders believe that they can still oppress and afflict. Those who do not know Jesus as Lord and Savior are especially vulnerable to their wickedness, however, even Christians are not completely exempt from demonic attacks.

Some attacks are simply arbitrary, but at times demons seek to attach to access points in our lives. These points can be places of habitual sin, places of deep emotional wounding, and especially places of bitterness and unforgiveness toward someone who hurt us. As a result, the inbreaking of the Father's love, which brings healing, repentance and release at the core of a person's life, can become a powerful tool in freeing someone from demonic affliction. Through my own experiences ministering to those who are oppressed, I have come to believe that the enemy often fixes his hold on the pains that were suffered early in life and the resulting unforgiveness stemming from them. Fathers Matthew and Dennis Linn, in their book *Deliverance Prayer,* tell how one effective deliverance ministry they were acquainted with found "that ninety percent of those having evil spirits have an open door due to deep hurts in life making it difficult to get close to Jesus."[5] Many times the core injury is a father issue that can only be resolved by the freeing touch of the Father's love.

Bill was a married, Christian man in his thirties. He loved to worship and faithfully helped the poor in the community. He maintained a cheerful public façade, but privately he was struggling with depression, a sense of distance from God and, most troubling of all, sexual impurity. He had become involved in pornography and cross-dressing, wearing a woman's clothing. The practice left him filled with guilt and shame. He had often "gone to the altar" and repented. He had also attended recovery groups, but his freedom was always short-lived. His recurring failure brought him to a place of hopelessness.

One evening I was with Bill at a small home fellowship where we shared Communion together. After the Lord's

Supper I strongly sensed the presence of Jesus and his desire to set Bill free. I went over and prayed for him. Once again he confessed his secret sin and asked the Lord to free him. As I was praying I discerned that there was an evil power contending with us. I cried out for Bill's deliverance. Immediately Bill told me that a memory from deep in his childhood had come vividly to mind. He described it to me: "I remember when I was a little boy. I was crying because my mother was putting a pair of girls' underpants on me. Often in my childhood she made it clear that she wanted a little girl and not a boy. I often wished that my dad would come and rescue me from her but she completely dominated him. He always seemed to be cowering in the shadows, never coming to my rescue."

As Bill wept, I wept with him. I showed him how to pray to forgive his mother for what she had done, and his dad for what he failed to do. When he was done I pronounced him forgiven for his hidden resentment toward his parents as well as his sexual immorality. I then prayed for his release from the stronghold of sin in his life. At that point a powerful demon that had been holding Bill in the stronghold of immorality manifested itself and challenged our authority to send it away. I proclaimed the power of the blood of Jesus over Bill's life and commanded the spirit to leave, and it did.

Once the demon left we invited the Father's love in to

heal the wound of Bill's emotional abandonment by his father. We asked the Father to deliver Bill from the false identification placed on him by his mother, and to re-identify him as a son. We asked the Father to fill him with the love that he had missed his entire life. The resultant river of love that the Father poured out flowed through him for hours, carrying away painful pockets of loneliness, guilt, shame, embarrassment, fear and self-hate. When all was said and done, Bill was free to rebuild his life, this time knowing that he was a son with a Father who loved him enough to come to his rescue.

Not every situation where someone struggles with chronic sinful behavior involves a demon; just as not every sickness is of demonic origin. However, there are times when the powers of darkness play a role, and when they do they must be driven out. When they have a foothold in the painful core issues of a person's life, the Father's love is often a very necessary component of deliverance. Deliverance ministry can become very complex; factors such as mental and physical health, spiritual history and maturity, and relational circles can all affect the situation. As a result, healing in this area sometimes requires the help of medical doctors, professional counselors and the prayer ministry of the church. The ministry of the Father's love is an important part of the overall healing process. Matthew and Dennis Linn offer some good general counsel:

Deliverance does not heal; it only provides the avenue through which healing can take place. And that healing is sealed by the action of God's love and the action of my love in Christ for that person. Only that love will convince such persons that they have not been abandoned by God. Only that love will preserve them from a damaging anxiety about themselves that may persist for the rest of their lives. Only that love diminishes the power of evil and shows it to be the sham that it really is.[6]

Rebuilding Broken Relationships

Frequently the most painful causes of suffering in our lives are broken relationships. When something goes wrong in a marriage, family or friendship, we need help and healing. Help can come in the form of good biblical insight that we can apply to our situation. It may come through sage advice from a mature friend or even a professional counselor. If we diligently apply what we have learned this kind of help may be sufficient, but sometimes the problems and painful suffering continue. This is usually because the emotions involved are too strong, and our personal resolve too weak. However, it is in such difficult situations that an experience of the Father's love can be of great help.

Many of our emotional issues and dysfunctional relational habits are directly tied to historic father issues that need to be healed at a deeper level. In fact, these deep core issues surface most in intimate relationships, where, out of love and the need to be loved, we have committed ourselves to a place of personal vulnerability. For example, if a man experienced rejection in his childhood, he might grow up with a heightened fear of rejection in other relationships. He may react negatively when someone tries to offer him constructive advice, causing a breakdown in that relationship. If this occurs in his marriage the pain can be heightened because of his emotional vulnerability to his wife. When this pattern becomes chronic, a crisis situation develops. In order to bring healing to such a situation, sound counsel for proper behavior must be given, and the love of the Father must be ministered to the historic injury of rejection.

Someone once said that opposites attract. The relationships that form on this principle can either have a dynamic, positive synergy or a negative dysfunction. This is very true in marriage. And I have often found that conflicts which occur in marriages are often a result of unresolved father issues. Here is a scenario I have seen repeated many times over: A man who has fearful insecurity issues because of his father's impossible demands marries a woman who has chronic guilt feelings and low self-esteem because her alcoholic father never gave her genuine affection and affirmation. (This is not a stereotypical male or female pattern; the fear or guilt issues could be reversed). The husband, due to his fears, becomes very controlling of his environment, including his wife. Due to her historic feelings of guilt, she obeys, even when she feels manipulated. Both partners, who are really desperate for intimacy and love, end up living in a dysfunctional game that prevents a real exchange of affection. The game can go on for quite a while until loneliness, frustration, hopelessness and resentment move the relationship into the crisis zone. The options of divorce or an extra-marital affair raise their ugly heads as one spouse or the other feels like the love is gone.

When the ship of marriage finally hits an iceberg, the painful emotions that violently surface threaten to sink the relationship. But these emotions are connected to the historic father issues that have been driving the dysfunction all along. This moment of emotional upheaval is very precarious, but it is the precise point where the Father's love can be introduced to the individuals in the relationship. We can see how this might work by continuing with the scenario above. If the husband received the Father's love, his fears could be reduced; from this new, more secure position he could set his wife free to be her own person and freely give her affectionate love. If she received the Father's love, her childhood void could be filled. Her sense of guilt could be washed away so that she could stand up straight in life with a real sense of self-worth. If each partner experienced the warmth of the Father's love flowing through them as they worked through the challenges of positive change, love could be rekindled.

The components differ from marriage to marriage, but when the Father's love becomes the common denominator in the equation of working through relational difficulties, many marriages become stronger then ever. The Father's love has tremendous potential to heal broken relationships because it brings healing to the deep historical problems, often painful father issues, that are causing the conflict, and frees people to really love one another. If we look closely at minor or major breakdowns in important relationships in our lives, we may find these same issues are part of the problem. Wherever the conflict arises: in the family unit, at work, and especially in the church, we may recognize a need for more of the Father's love. In fact, our relationship with the Father in heaven is strongly connected to our relationships here on earth. Breakdowns in our earthly relationships can force us to look at the core issues of our lives and thus facilitate our discovery of the Father's love for us. The flow of the Father's love into our lives shows us how to love each other. As the Apostle John wrote, "We love because he first loved us" (1 John 4:19).

Now when we look at the various ways we can suffer in this life, be it from physical affliction, emotional pain, demonic oppression or relational breakdown, perhaps we can see how the Father of all compassion wants to help us and heal us. At the same time, we can understand that through our suffering our Father in heaven can open our eyes to his great love for us, which is the greatest healing there is. The "children's bread" is wonderful, but the eternal love of our Father is the best thing of all.

8

PARADIGM SHIFT

"Only if we allow ourselves to be kindled by the love of the Father's heart and then this very day look around for those to whom we can apply this love ... only if we enter into this living circuit of divine love and let it warm us and flow through us will it suddenly become clear to us what it means and what a joy it is to know the fatherly heart in heaven." – Helmut Thielicke

I directed my eyes up to the overhead screen where a black and white image was projected. The speaker behind the podium asked how many in the audience saw an old hag. I raised my hand, along with many others. Then he asked how many could see a beautiful woman. I squinted hard until all of a sudden I saw her and raised my hand. I realized that I could see either figure in the same drawing, depending on what I was looking for. The speaker used the exercise to illustrate the concept of a "paradigm shift":

141

shifting your point of view based on new information or new experience. He explained that we can have paradigm shifts in our Christian experience. After years of being very conservative concerning the ministry of the Holy Spirit, I received a powerful infilling of the Spirit and teaching on the use of spiritual gifts today. As a result I began to see the Holy Spirit's working in the pages of the Bible as never before. Examples just jumped off the page during my morning devotions. I saw the Spirit working in my life through the use of his gifts. I saw him working in the lives of those around me in supernatural ways. I had experienced a "paradigm shift" concerning the Holy Spirit.

Meeting the Father and experiencing his love produces a paradigm shift in our lives. All of a sudden we begin to see the Father in our Christian experience in a new way. As we read the Bible we see references to his love that we just seemed to overlook before. The knowledge of his love unlocks new meaning in old, familiar passages. For example, I John 3:1 has new and deeper meaning after experiencing the Father's love: "How great is the love the Father has lavished on us, that we should be called children of God!"

The presence of the Father with us causes us to see the disciplines and dynamics of our Christian life in the light of his love. I am not saying that we disregard our relationship with our Lord Jesus or the ministry of the Holy Spirit; those maintain their importance even as the Father takes his proper place in our lives. Jesus said that if we love him, both he and the Father will come and make their home within us (John 14:23). And when the Father's presence rests within us we see his love at work in a whole new way. His love effects a paradigm shift in our study of the Word of God, our worship, the working out of our sanctification and our witness to the world. We find that we can experience more of his love as we pursue these activities, and that this same love empowers a new effectiveness in doing them.

The Word of God

Our study of the Bible provides the sure foundation for our spiritual growth, and we can apply this truth to our deepening relationship with the Father and the ongoing experience of his love. The inbreaking love of the Father causes us to appreciate every reference to God the Father in a new way. We see his love at work in the pages of scripture as never before. I now see the Father's love motivating Creation in the book of Genesis, culminating history in the Revelation, and flowing in all the events in between. Each page can contain a new discovery of some aspect of his love. In the Old Testament direct references to the Father are rare but rich. Take, for example, Isaiah 63:16: "But you are our Father, though Abraham does not know us or Israel acknowledge us; you, O Lord are our Father, our Redeemer from of old is your name." Some verses disclose the nature of his affectionate love through comparisons to a mother's love (Isaiah 49:15). One of my favorites to meditate on is Psalm 103:13: "As a father has compassion on his children, so the Lord has compassion on those who fear him."

The Hebrew word translated here as "compassion" is *racham.* Strong's Concordance defines this word as tender love, based upon the image of a womb gently embracing a developing fetus.[1] When this term for compassion is used in the Old Testament, it is describing the incredibly intimate embrace of the Father's love. For years I missed the deeper meaning of the word compassion; now I weep every time I read it.

In the New Testament the revelation of the Father breaks forth dramatically on many pages. This is a direct result of the ministry of the Lord Jesus Christ, who came expressly to reveal the Father and his love (Luke 10:22). The Gospel of John makes the Father a primary focus. John begins early, telling us that Jesus had come to help us know the Father in greater intimacy and mercy. The love of the Father unfolds in declarations such as the famous John 3:16, and is defined as demonstrated natural affection in John 16:27. The Apostle Paul reinforces these themes in his letters. He reveals the Father as the great source of compassion in 2 Corinthians 1:3 and describes the inbreaking of that compassionate love in Romans 8:15–16. Scriptures like these are essential in renewing our minds and solidifying our absolute belief that the Father loves us. They also become avenues for the Spirit to visit us and touch us afresh with the reality of that same love.

Worshipping the Father

In the late 1980's I was a session speaker at a conference in Canada featuring John Wimber. During one of the sessions taught by a colleague, I noticed that the worship team played songs at the end of the message that seemed to facilitate the Holy Spirit's ministry to the responding people. When I finished my own session I asked the worship leader, Andy Park, if he had a fitting song about the Father's love. He told me that his guitar player might have just the song for the occasion. The young electric guitar player unfolded a piece of paper with a freshly written song on it. He set it at his feet, looked down and began to play. These were the first words I heard as the Spirit fell, and I felt the Father's presence:

Father, I want you to hold me
I want to rest in your arms today

Father, I want you to show me
How much you care for me in every way
I bring all my cares and I lay them at your feet
You are always there
And you love me as I am, yes, you love me as I am[2]

The young man's name was Brian Doerksen, and he would go on to write many songs that lead us into the Father's presence. What I have never forgotten since that day is that when we worship the Father, he responds by drawing us to himself and touching us with his love.

Jesus taught us that the day was coming when we would worship the Father in spirit and truth (John 4:23). To worship him means to enter intimately into his presence with reverence. As we meet with our Father he draws us to his breast, to that place Jesus has prepared for us (John 1:18), and there we receive his tender affections. This happens in our times of private devotion and even increases in our public times of corporate worship. Fortunately, the Lord Jesus has anointed many worship songwriters, such as Brian and my longtime travel companion John Barnett, to bring forth songs that lead the church to the Father. The Father is faithful to visit his children wherever these songs are sung. In my life the greatest source of ongoing renewal of the Father's love is worship, whether I'm listening to a CD in the quiet of my home or standing in the first row of our church sanctuary, lifting up my voice in song to the Father.

When we worship the Father we not only grow in our love relationship with him, but we find ourselves worshipping Jesus in an ever-deeper way. We come to taste of the love with which the Father loved the Son. The love we receive from the Father is then poured out at the feet of Jesus. We learn to love Jesus with demonstrated affection and thus with all our body, soul and spirit. As we continually receive the love that is given to us by God our Father we find ourselves falling more and more in love with Jesus. This dynamic is very important in maintaining our first love for Jesus (Revelation 2:4). Many people whose fervent love for Jesus has waned over the years have rediscovered it through the experience of the Father's love.

Working Out Our Sanctification

Sanctification is a big word that describes the lifelong process of becoming more and more like Christ, becoming holy as he is holy. We embark upon this road of change when we receive Jesus as Lord and Savior. We come to its end when Jesus takes us home into glory. The time in between is both challenging and rewarding. Knowing the Father and experiencing his love is absolutely essential to completing our course and reaching our full potential in serving God. Our Lord Jesus gives us the perfect model of what our lives are to look like in character and conduct. His own life was one of obedience to his Father whom he knew loved him. At his baptism that love initiated his public service, and in Gethsemane that same love sustained him as he faced his approaching death on the cross. Our sanctification is greatly helped when it is initiated with the love of Father and then daily sustained by that same love.

The Apostle Paul addresses the Christians in Colossi as God's chosen people, holy and dearly loved (Colossians 3:14). Our experience of the love of God both motivates and helps to maintain our holiness. Without being secured by the love of the Father, it is easy for us to drift into the position of trying to be holy in order to somehow merit the Father's love. That usually leads to religious posturing, false facades and self-condemnation. Ken Blue once shared with me that it is difficult to righteously fulfill the imperatives found in the New Testament without having experienced the Father's love. I took this to mean that without the movement of God's love in our hearts we can end up turning the commands of scripture into religious works. The Father's love fills our insecurities, frees us from religious tendencies and facilitates a healthy motivation for holiness. We want to be holy because we want to stay relationally centered in the Father's love. When we drift into sin we feel separated from God, but that same love motivates a sincere repentance that quickly reinstates us to our love relationship with the Father.

One of the greatest challenges in the process of sanctification is obeying the Lord's commands to us when it is hard to do so. Circumstances in our lives can stir up our insecurities to the point where we are afraid to go forward in following Jesus. Jesus faced just such a fearful situation in the garden of Gethsemane on the dark night before his crucifixion. There, deeply distressed, he prayed to his Father that the hour might pass from him. In other words, going forward in obedience to his Father was extremely difficult. The Gospel of Mark reveals the dramatic encounter with the Father that enabled him to go on: "'Abba, Father,' he said, 'everything is possible for you. Take this cup from me. Yet not what I will, but what you will'" (Mark 14:36).

Jesus had an intimate, and I believe loving, Abba Father experience. The result is that he was comforted and gained confidence to meet the most demanding requirement in fulfilling his Father's will: going to the cross. This event offers us a pattern to follow when we face the challenge of obedience. At those moments when our deepest fears rise up to halt our forward movement, we need to draw near to the Father and let his perfect love deliver us from our fears, freeing us to follow him fully. It is in following fully that we continue to set our lives apart for

God and in the process are sanctified.

I have a good friend named Tom. We were reunited several years ago after a period of estrangement. The death of a friend we had in common drew us together, as we both spoke and he sang at the memorial service. Tom selected a song that spoke of the comfort of being a child of God, and the Spirit of the Father anointed him as he sang. After observing this move of the Spirit, I invited Tom to accompany me to one of my conferences and to sing about the Father's love. A few months later Tom performed a moving song titled "The Father's Chair," which chronicles our search to sit in our Father's lap, embraced in his love. As Tom sang, not only was nearly everyone in tears, but he himself was so overwhelmed by the Father's love for him that he needed help standing in order to finish the song. Over the following years Tom sang to thousands, and each time was flooded with the Father's love.

Two years ago, Tom went to the doctor to have a small lump inspected. Days later he was reeling under the diagnosis of widespread cancer of the prostate, with a matter of months to live. As you can imagine these last two years have been difficult, but through it all Tom's relationship with his heavenly Father has remained strong. The knowledge of the Father's love has bolstered his confidence to believe the best and fight the disease with faith. More importantly, his experience of the Father's love comforts him in his most frightening hours. When he feels up to it he joins our worship band on stage at church and sings songs to the Father. The Father's love falls afresh on him and overflows to all of us. He radiates the holy presence of Jesus wherever he goes. Many of the people who draw near to help him experience some measure of healing in their own lives.

Tom's life is a beautiful example of a sanctified life shaped by adversity from without and the Father's sustaining love within. Just as love enabled our Lord Jesus to lay his life down for others, Tom has been enabled by the Father's love to face his illness and, like Jesus, give his life away, bringing many home to the Father. Working out our sanctification is essentially learning how to become like Jesus; learning how to be loved by our Father and laying our lives down in service to others. Tom's life demonstrates this dynamic lived out in the face of great difficulty. He is a model to you and I.

Closely connected to obedience to the Father is responding correctly when he allows us to encounter difficulties in order to produce holiness in our lives. We must remember that our Father is still there loving us at those times. The writer of the book of Hebrews puts it this way:

And you have forgotten that word of encouragement that addresses you as sons: "My son, do not make light of the Lord's discipline, and do not lose

heart when he rebukes you, because the Lord disciplines those he loves, and he punishes everyone he
accepts as a son" (Hebrews 12:5, 6).

The knowledge and experience of the Father's love is crucial in enduring and profiting from adverse situations.
The Father perfects his love and holiness in our lives by
allowing us to face difficulties that cause our core fears
and foolish sinful habits to come to the surface of our
lives so that they can be removed by the power of his love.
Without the experiential reality of the Father's love, one
may react negatively to the shaping work of his hands and
lose the benefit of adversity.

Witnessing to the World

As Christians we are well aware of the necessity of fulfilling the Great Commission by spreading the good news
about Jesus and leading people into discipleship. When we
experience the love of the Father, a paradigm shift takes
place in this witness. We see how important the Father's
love is, both in the content of the gospel message and the
spirit in which it is given. Thomas Smail comments:

We have had in recent years a Jesus movement and
a charismatic movement. The one has almost disappeared and the other is threatening to run out of
steam, perhaps because each is in a different way

inadequate to the gospel, which is basically a Father movement. … It starts not with the cross of Jesus or with the gift of the Spirit, but with the Father who so loved the world that he gave his Son in his Spirit.[3]

The evidence of this is found in the classic evangelistic text, John 3:16: "For God so loved the world that he gave his one and only Son, that whoever believes in him shall not perish but have eternal life." When we have seen the face of the Father in our lives we see that it was he, acting as Father, who sent Jesus to us, and his love was the motivation. When we simply tell someone that the Father loves them and that he sent Jesus to save them so that they might become his beloved children, we bring a timely word to a world searching for the Father's love. The mere mention of a loving Father often softens hearts toward the Gospel.

Even more importantly, the love of the Father enables us to witness to the world in a spirit of compassion. Jesus' ministry was driven by compassion. Henri Nouwen takes notice of this in Jesus' ministry to Lazarus:

There is a love story here. Lazarus was one of Jesus' closest friends, and his deep compassion for Lazarus's sisters, as well as his great love for Lazarus, moved Jesus to call Lazarus back to life. Whenever Jesus calls someone to life – the son of the widow of

Nain, the daughter of Jairus – we always see an immense love and compassion. It is this love and compassion that is the source of new life.[4]

The word compassion comes from two Latin words, *cum* and *pati,* which mean "to suffer with." The Greek word describing Jesus' ministry is *splanchnon,* translated in the King James Version as the "bowels of mercy," where the deepest emotions were thought to reside, particularly those of affection. Combining these terms, we can describe compassion as caring for those in need motivated by deep feelings of affectionate concern for them. It is sharing the heart of the Father for them. Jesus was well equipped to be compassionate because he himself had been touched by his Father's compassionate love at his baptism. The flow of the Father's compassion through us is initiated and sustained by our experience of his love.

The Gospel accounts show us that whenever Jesus was moved with compassion to help, the power of God was manifest to heal. The principle catalyst for the powerful signs and wonders that accompanied Jesus' ministry was compassion. His ministry was one of "empowered compassion." That dynamic has not changed today. When we are moving with the Father's heart of compassion we will also find ourselves seeing signs and wonders confirming God's reality to a lost world. This is of critical importance in evangelizing the world today. Where the strongholds of darkness are obvious, as in many Third World countries, a Gospel with accompanying signs and wonders is absolutely necessary.

The need for this "empowered compassion" is just as great in First World countries like the United States. With contemporary western society demonstrating a heightened interest in compassion for those suffering from abuse, prejudice, and diseases such as AIDS, it is imperative that the church not only present the moral truth of the Bible, but also demonstrate the "empowered compassion" of the Father. As we head towards the new Millennium the true compassion of God the Father must flow out of our hearts to the world we are trying to reach. There is a fatherless generation growing daily across the face of the earth and even across the street from where you live. They are searching for the Father's love. We who have received his love have the responsibility to share it with them.

Epilogue

"E.T. phone home! E.T. phone home!" These are memorable words from one of the most popular motion pictures Hollywood has ever made. E.T. was the story of a little alien creature who was stranded on earth, with a deep desire to return home to the place where he belonged. In a famous scene E.T. is sending signals over a radio device he has made and the kids who befriended him ask him what he is doing. He responds with the words I quoted; he is trying to phone home. There is a happy end to the story because his call is received and he is rescued. He gets back home to where he belongs.

We too, have a deep desire to return to that place where we belong, that place where we are loved for who we are. It is a desire that God our Father has sovereignly placed deep within us. Something in us longs to be with him, held in his loving embrace and at home in his house. So, beginning early in life we search for the Father's love. We keep "phoning home." We look for love from our natural fathers and may or may nor find it. We "dial up" the pleasures of the world or heroic performances to find it, but it is not there. Our makeshift devices don't seem to be working. Then, all of a sudden, the Father begins to ring our number. If we make the connection he speaks to us and begins to direct us home. There we find him waiting with arms outstretched to welcome us into the warm embrace of his love. Our deepest desire is satisfied.

I have a good friend named Steve who is a policeman in Santa Ana, California. He tells a story about a man named Albert. It is a story of homecoming. Here is how Steve tells it:

> It was a warm Thursday evening in June. I was on patrol in my black and white police car, working the busy summertime streets in Santa Ana. As I was driving down a major city street, my attention was drawn to a man at a pay phone in a darkened parking lot. He appeared to be what I can only describe as water-skiing with the phone: he had the phone in both of his hands and was leaning backwards at a 45 degree angle, holding on with all his might and extending the phone cord to its limit. I thought this was a bit odd, but I've seen much stranger things in this city, and besides, I was working on a higher priority investigation, so I kept on driving. But the Lord had other priorities in mind for me. No sooner had I driven an extra couple of blocks than the Lord told me I needed to speak to the man at the phone. So, a quick U-turn and thirty seconds later I was back at the pay phone and about to meet Albert.

Albert was still water-skiing with the phone as I parked my police car behind him. I called out to him, "Excuse me, sir, but I don't think Ma Bell would appreciate you doing pull-ups with one of her pay phones!" As Albert turned around and our eyes met, the warning bells went off. This was a hard-core bad guy! Albert had "the LOOK." After years of street patrol, you can tell when you're dealing with a petty criminal and when you're dealing with an experienced ex-felon on parole. Albert was one of the latter. He had prison tattoos on his neck, arms, and body. He was muscular, although he appeared to have recently lost some weight. His face displayed little, if any, emotion. And his arms showed a long history of narcotic usage. I thought, "Lord, why have you placed me before this man?" as I quickly checked Albert for any concealed weapons. I was soon to find out.

I began speaking with Albert, asking what he was doing with the phone. Albert said he was trying to make a phone call but was having trouble getting through, so while waiting to try again, he thought he'd exercise with the phone. He went on to tell me that he'd been out of prison for about five months. I could sense that the Lord was urging me to continue speaking to Albert, so I did, asking about his life and how he ended up in a life of crime.

Albert then went on to share his life story. He was 13 years old when his father kicked him out of the house onto the streets, telling Albert he could no longer afford to care for him as well as the several younger children in the house. Albert's eyes were focused on a far away time and place as he shared that painful moment with me. Soon after hitting the streets he began stealing food. He was still just 13 years old when he began using heroin, and his food stealing progressed to commercial burglaries to support his drug habit. At the age of 21, he was sentenced to state prison. While there, he "did some bad things" which cost him an additional 19 years in a maximum-security prison. He contracted HIV, which by the time I met him had progressed to the second stage of AIDS. This explained his thinness, and I could see the familiar sunken features in his face. He had been released on parole a few months before and was living in a nearby halfway house.

As Albert shared his life story with me, I saw before me not a hardened criminal, but a desperate, discarded, dying man. The new eyes, ears, and heart that my Lord has given me are at odds nowadays with my old fleshly self, the one which a short season ago would've shunned this disease infested criminal. Instead, compassion welled up inside me. For a moment, the Lord let me see Albert through the eyes of his son Jesus.

I decided to go deep. "Are you ready to die, Albert?" I asked. He answered that some days he wanted to die. I asked if he knew where he'd go when he died. Albert never hesitated. "Yes, I'm going to hell," he answered. "I think God will chain my hands over my head and keep me there for a long, long time."

I knew then why the Lord had placed me in this situation, and I quietly prayed, asking for more courage, strength and wisdom. I spoke to Albert no longer as a policeman, but as a Christian saved by grace. I started by sharing with him what the Bible says about the finality and eternity of hell. Then I told Albert that, as he was sharing about his childhood, I saw that he was still hurting over the way his father had abandoned him. Albert looked me in the eyes, his expression one of bewilderment, as if to say, "Where are you going with this?" Then his expression changed, his eyes looking through me again as he thought back to when he was thirteen. "I really wasn't such a bad kid then," he allowed, "yeah, it hurt a lot."

That was when I shared the Father's love with Albert. I told him that although his father here on earth abandoned him, I knew of a Father who would NEVER abandon him, NEVER leave him alone, NEVER lie to him, and who ALWAYS has and will love him. I watched in amazement as this 40 year old man, a man who had done things he couldn't even speak about, looked at me with eyes filling with huge tears. He didn't speak, he just stood there crying.

I reached into my duty bag and withdrew several tracts I carry. I gave these to Albert and asked him to read them and consider seriously making a commitment for Jesus. Albert said he would and thanked me, then I climbed back into my patrol car and started down the road again. I thought I had completed me assigned mission for the Lord. So much for my thinking!

I drove down the street, getting exactly as far as I had before, only to have the Lord tell me, "YOU ARE NOT FINISHED YET!" I drove back into the lot and there was Albert, holding onto the phone again, and reading one of the tracts. This time he saw me coming and placed the phone on the receiver as he walked over to me. He seemed genuinely happy to talk to me again. I shared more of the Good News with Albert, telling him that no matter what he'd ever done – even the stuff he couldn't talk about – God already knew about it. Once again, Albert began weeping. I asked him if he knew about Jesus. Wiping more tears away, Albert answered that he'd read a little about him from a prison Bible. I told Albert that Jesus was standing there with us and that he wanted to come into his life, to fill him with love, forgiveness, and acceptance. I told Albert that it only required a sincere heart, one willing to believe in Jesus Christ as Lord and Savior. I asked him if he wanted to invite Jesus into his life. Albert answered, "Yes." A few minutes later I was speaking to a new brother in Christ. The tears now flowed from us both. Tears of joy, of a lost one found, of a prodigal returned home. I knew I had completed my mission this time.

However, before I drove away again, there was one more question I wanted to ask Albert. "Just who was it that you were so desperate to call, Albert?" I asked. He smiled and told me, "I was trying to call long distance to my father. I haven't spoken to him in years. I wanted to talk to him one more time before I die."

The story of Steve and Albert parallels the themes of this book: our search for the love of a father, the discovery of the Father's love, and the move to share that love with the prodigals who cross the paths of our lives. This story also depicts the different places we might find ourselves in at this very moment. Where do you see yourself right now? Have you been "phoning home?" Have you been searching for the Father's love but have not yet found it? My prayer is that the message in this book would help you make the connection, help you to realize how much the Father loves you and reveal to you the pathway home. Even here and now, you can lift up your prayer to the Father, in the name of Jesus, and he will answer from heaven. His love can flow into your heart just as it did with Albert and all those whose stories were told in this book.

Steve's story also reminds me afresh of where the experience of the Father's love leads us. The heart of the Father beating in us moves us to share his love with all those lost prodigals searching for love. Many are "phoning home" around us. The Father wants to use you and I to help them make the connection with him. My prayer is that those of us who have so richly received the Father's love would take it to the streets, just as Steve did. May the Holy Spirit fill us afresh and send us on this mission of love.

Notes

Chapter 1

1. John Martin, *Author Looks at Modern Fatherhood,* Knight-Ridder/Tribune News Service, 18 September 1996

2. David Blankenhorn, *Fatherless America* (New York: Basic Books, 1995), 1.

3. Blankenhorn, 2-3.

4. Thomas A. Smail, *The Forgotten Father* (London: Paternoster Press, 1996), 19-20, 21.

5. J. I. Packer, *Knowing God* (Illinois: InterVarsity Press, 1973), 207.

6. Packer, 182.

7. Charles F. Stanley, "Emotional Baggage in the Ministry," *Christian Counseling Today,* January 1993, 35.

Chapter 2

1. "Nowhere in the entire wealth of devotional literature produced by ancient Judaism do we find *'abba'* being used as a way of addressing God. The pious Jew knew too much of the great gap between God and man (Eccl. 5:1) to be free to address God with the familiar word used in everyday family life. ... The entirely

new, and for Jews unheard of, use of the childish and familiar term *'abba'* in prayer is an expression of the unique relationship of Jesus to God" (Colin Brown, ed., *The New International Dictionary of New Testament Theology* [Grand Rapids: Zondervan Publishing House, 1979], 614, 615).

2. W. E. Vine, *An Expository Dictionary of New Testament Words,* vol. 3, *Lo-Ser* (New Jersey: Fleming H. Revell Company, 1966), 21.

3. Norval Geldenhuys, *Commentary on the Gospel of Luke* (Grand Rapids: Wm. B. Eerdmans Publishing Company, 1977), 146, 147.

4. John Nolland provides an excellent discussion of these terms in the *Word Biblical Commentary,* vol. 35A, Luke 1–9:20 (Dallas: Word Books, 1989), 162–165.

5. Henri Nouwen, *Here and Now* (New York: Crossroad Publishing Company, 1995), 100.

6. B. F. Westcott, *The Gospel According to St. John* (Grand Rapids: Wm. B. Eerdmans Publishing Company, 1978), 248.

Chapter 3

1. James D. G. Dunn, *Word Biblical Commentary,* vol. 38A, Romans 1–8 (Dallas: Word Books, 1988), 265.

2. J. Gilchrist Lawson, *Deeper Experiences of Famous Christians* (Indiana: Warner Press, 1972), 180.

3. Clark H. Pinnock, *Flame of Love* (Illinois: InterVarsity Press, 1996), 87, 133, 166.

4. Pinnock, 149, 153, 155.

5. Dunn, 452.

6. H. A. Ironside, *Lectures on the Epistle to the Romans* (New Jersey: Loizeaux Brothers, Inc., 1978), 102.

7. Henri Nouwen, *Bread for the Journey* (San Francisco: HarperCollins Publishers, 1997), June 12.

8. Dunn, 461.

9. D. M. Lloyd-Jones, *Romans: The Sons of God* (Grand Rapids: Zondervan Publishing House, 1975), 241.

10. Dunn, 462.

11. Lloyd-Jones, 235–236.

12. Dunn, 462.

13. Lloyd-Jones, 245.

Chapter 4

1. Henri Nouwen, *Bread for the Journey* (San Francisco: HarperCollins Publishers, 1997), June 30.

2. Philip Yancey, *What's So Amazing About Grace?* (Grand Rapids: Zondervan Publishing House, 1997), 203.

3. Henri Nouwen, *The Return of the Prodigal Son* (New York: Doubleday, 1992), 38–39.

4. Helmut Thielicke, *The Waiting Father* (San Francisco: Harper & Row Publishers, 1959), 26.

Chapter 5

1. Henri Nouwen, *The Return of the Prodigal Son* (New York: Doubleday, 1992), 66–67.

Chapter 6

1. Michael Phillips, *A God to Call Father* (Wheaton: Tyndale House Publishers, 1994), 105.
2. Phillips, 101, 104–105.
3. John Nolland, *Word Biblical Commentary,* vol. 35B, Luke 9:21–18:34 (Dallas: Word Books, 1993), 632.
4. Phillips, 103–104.
5. Gordon Dalbey, *Father and Son* (Nashville: Thomas Nelson Publishers, 1992), 128.
6. Henri Nouwen, *Sabbatical Journey* (New York: Crossroad Publishing Company, 1998), 130.

Chapter 7

1. Francis MacNutt, *Healing* (Notre Dame: Ave Maria Press, 1984), 171.
2. W. Hugh Missildine, *Your Inner Child of the Past* (New York: Pocket Books, 1982), 4.
3. Gary Smalley & John Trent, *The Blessing* (Nashville: Thomas Nelson Publishers, 1986), 117.
4. Smalley & Trent, 158, 159.

5. Matthew & Dennis Linn, *Deliverance Prayer* (New York: Paulist Press, 1981), 162.
6. Linn, 203.

Chapter 8

1. James Strong, *The New Strong's Exhaustive Concordance of the Bible: Dictionary of the Hebrew Bible* (Nashville: Thomas Nelson Publishers, 1990), 108.
2. Brian Doerksen, "Father, I Want You to Hold Me," Mercy/Vineyard Publishing, 1989
3. Thomas A. Smail, *The Forgotten Father* (London: Paternoster Press, 1996), 20.
4. Henri Nouwen, *Sabbatical Journey* (New York: Crossroad Publishing Company, 1998), 133.

ED PIOREK

THE

CENTRAL

event

EXPERIENCING THE POWER OF THE FATHER'S LOVE

PRODUCT PAGE

The Central Event – Book

Five years after writing his best-selling *The Father Loves You,* Ed Piorek takes a deeper look at the Father's love in his life. His recent victory over cancer revealed the Father's compassion for him as never before. He shares the lessons learned about living a life that depends on, rests in and ministers out of the power of the Father's love.

Essential Manhood – Book

Join Ed as he explores the desires of every man for personal, marital and family success and the difference the discovery of the Father's love makes in reaching it. It is filled with true, humorous life stories that everyone – both male and female – can identify with.

The Father Loves You Conference 2004 – CD Set

Listen to Ed and Janet Piorek share their most recent teaching on the Father's love. The classic themes of the Revelation of the Father's Love and the Restoration of the Father Relationship are renewed with deepened insight after Ed's recovery from cancer. The section on the Return of the Prodigal Son is completely new with rich imagery drawn from Rembrandt's famous painting by the same name. This digitally mastered set includes an illustrated syllabus.

The Father Loves You Video Teaching Series – DVD set

After twenty years of worldwide ministry on the Father's love, Ed Piorek shares his experiences and insights with a small group of international pastors. Join in this intimate classroom setting as Ed instructs and interacts on many aspects of the Father's love with men and women just like you. Sessions include his timeless testimony, newest teaching on the central event of Jesus' baptism and spiritual fathering.

ORDERS: www.fatherlovesyou.com

E-MAIL: vcfmv@att.net

BOOK ORDERS

Name ....

Address ....

Title/s ....

....

Author/s .... Quantity ....

Books can be ordered from the following
Vineyard International Publishing distributors:

Australia
P.O. Box 483
South Hurstville
NSW 2221
Fax: +61 2 9547 2380
Tel: +61 2 9547 3911
hangingd@hangingduck.com

Benelux
P.O. Box 1557,
3500 BN Utrecht,
The Netherlands
Fax: +31 30 2340958
books@vineyard.nl

Canada
Peter Fitch
13 Main St
St Stephen
New Brunswick, E3L 1Y7
pfitch@nbnet.nb.ca

England
Ed & Clare Evans
22 Park Street, Salisbury, SP1 3AU
Tel: +44 1722 326885
edevans@talk21.com

New Zealand
VMG Aotearoa NZ
116 Wairere Rd
Waitakere, Auckland, NZ
vmg-anz@vineyard.co.nz

Norway
Oyvind Nerheim, Oslo Vineyard
St Halvardsgt.20
0192, Oslo, Norway
Tel: +47 24070707
nerheim@vineyard.no

South Africa
P.O. Box 53286, Kenilworth 7745
Tel & Fax: +27 21 6712633
vip@vineyardbi.org
www.vineyardbi.org/vip

Sweden
Krister Burstrom
Din Bok i Skelleftea
Stationsgatan 12
931 31 Skelleftea
krister@dinbok.net

Switzerland/Austria/Germany
Mathew Mathai
Wehntalerstrasse 276
8046-Zurich, Switzerland
Tel: +41 1 371 7151
Fax: +41 1 371 7150
mathew@vineyard.ch

USA
AVC USA
5015 Grove West Blvd.
Stafford, Texas, 77477
deanna@vineyardusa.org